HERAKLES

HERAKLES

BY

GEORGE CABOT LODGE

BOSTON AND NEW YORK
HOUGHTON MIFFLIN COMPANY
The Riverside Press Cambridge
1908

Published November 1908

". . . AMPHITRYON, banished from Tiryns, established himself at Thebes. Herakles, brought up in that city and skilful in physical exercises, surpassed all other men in the strength of his body and the greatness of his soul. He was scarcely adolescent when he delivered Thebes [from the tyranny of Erginus and the Minyans], and thus paid his debt of gratitude to his country. . . . The fame of this exploit spread through the whole of Greece, and every one admired it as a prodigy. Creon, the King, himself impressed by the courage of the young man, gave him his daughter Megara in marriage; and, treating him like his own son, confided to him the government of his kingdom. But Eurystheus, King of Argos, jealous of the growth of the power of Herakles, summoned him to appear before him, and ordered him to perform his labours. At first Herakles refused, but Zeus commanded him to obey Eurystheus. Herakles went to Delphi, and, having consulted the oracle, he was told that the Gods ordered him to perform the twelve labours, and that, after their completion, he would receive immortality.

"On receiving this command, Herakles fell into great distress [of mind] . . . he was seized with a frenzy. . . . Madness took possession of his sick mind . . . in one of his ecstasies of fury, . . . Herakles pierced with arrows the children which he had had by Megara. . . .

Having recovered from his madness and become aware of his error, he was greatly afflicted by the excess of his misfortune . . . he remained quietly withdrawn in his house for a long time, avoiding all human society. Time having calmed his grief, Herakles went to Eurystheus, determined to affront every peril [and perform the labours]. . . .

"Zeus kept Prometheus chained for having given fire to mankind, and caused his heart to be devoured by an eagle. Herakles, seeing that Prometheus was punished only for having done good to men, . . . saved the common benefactor."

Diodorus Siculus, iv, 10–11, and 15.

CHARACTERS

HERAKLES
MEGARA, his wife
AMPHITRYON, his father
ALCMENA, his mother
IOLAUS, his nephew
THE THREE SONS OF HERAKLES (in infancy)
THE POET
THE WOMAN
CREON, King of Thebes, father of MEGARA
THE MESSENGER OF EURYSTHEUS
TEIRESIAS
THE PYTHIA, at the Temple of Apollo at Delphi
THE PROPHETES at the Temple of Apollo at Delphi
PROMETHEUS

also

MEN AND HARLOTS FROM THE TAVERN
THE CHORUS OF RESPONDENTS, in the Temple of Zeus at Thebes
THE CHORUS OF WORSHIPPERS, before the Temple of Apollo at Delphi
THE CHORUS OF OLD MEN, before the Temple of Hera at Thebes

also

Guests at the King's feast, Populace, Soldiers, Messengers, Slaves, etc.

FIRST SCENE

The Agora at Thebes. Sunset.

The Agora is empty except for the WOMAN, who is seated on a bench against the wall of a house, and the POET, who stands before her, facing the sunset.

HERAKLES

FIRST SCENE

The POET

The birds go home at sunset, and my heart
Goes home. The day closes its tired wings,
And in the violet evening there are stars
And silence.....And the best there was to do,
The best of us we left undone to-day,
Now like a warrior worn with doubtful wars,
Waits for the morrow, heart-sick yet resolved.
The sense of life is secret and serene
At twilight, and the flame of life —

The WOMAN

Is love!

The POET turns as tho' suddenly recalled to a sense of her presence, and looks at her for a moment in silence.

The POET

Of old your eyes persuade the heart like peril.....
You are the Siren of the seas of life.
What stately ships, full-sailed for Paradise,
Captained by young, superb adventurers,
Haughty in hope, impassioned in resolve,

HERAKLES

Thrilled with a mystic wonder in the mind,
Drawn from their course, lie shipwrecked on your
shores! —
What is your wish with me? I saw your eyes
Call to my heart across the crowded square.
Now in the sunset all the crowd is gone.
We are alone. Why did you summon me?

A moment's pause.

The WOMAN

You are but newly come into the city?

The POET

Since yesterday.

The WOMAN

What race and place are yours?

The POET

In Athens was I born, and there my youth
Was spent, and there, if home there be, is home.

The WOMAN

Why are you come to Thebes? What hope of good,
What fear of ill impels your feet so far?

The POET

My hope is nameless, and the ills I dread
Are housed within me! — but the restless mind

FIRST SCENE

While there is life, affords us no reprieve;
The impatient heart, eagerly and beyond
The daybreak and the dark, drives us afar
Over strange oceans and unvisited lands.....

The WOMAN

The impatient heart! — O Heart of man that yearns
After the Stranger Woman of young dreams!.....

The POET

I know! I know! — young dreams!.....But mine are old,
Tragic and old, divine and real as life,
And dwell within me like a visitation
Of Truth's unconquerable and mystic hope
Whereof no part is the flushed heart's desire.
What tho' — as inwardly my blood believes —
You were the Stranger Woman —

The WOMAN

I am She!
And anciently and now I am the one
Inveterate quest of life's dream-haunted days.
In myriad ways you seek me, and you find
Me! — tho' you think to find a lordlier thing.
Yet, tho' you find me, you shall know me not,
And I am strange to you forever!

HERAKLES

The POET

To me
Nothing of you is strange — unless your name!
I have had many lives before, where you
Were something more to me than life itself;
And after all my youth's vexed years with you,
I know you and your secret — and the soul
Within you, dark and undivined, I know!
I am so long possessed of you I seem
To have you as I have the voice of song,
Clear in my heart and brain. There is no phrase
Of laughter or desire or lamentation
In all the tones and tremors of your voice,
Various as wind, no silver gayeties,
No cries, tense and tear-laden, strange to me.
There is no perfume, bounty, brilliancy
Or pleasure of your body, nor the least
Stir of your subtle silks I know not of.
I know the grave, smooth silence of your brows;
And when your lips are eloquent and flushed
With hunger and with thirst of love, I know you!
I know the swift, sweet motion of your hands
When they are fain of touch and tenderness.....
And I have long explored and learned to know
The deep, dark twilights of your eyes and hair,
The young, pale profile of your breasts — and how
You are all warm and lustrous and superb!
Neither within the house of ivory,

FIRST SCENE

The house of rose and pearl, am I a stranger:
Your thought is in my brain, your mighty heart
Is in my heart, — your soul is in my soul!
I know the chaste reluctance and the wild
Appeal of the indomitable desire
When life is given entire as love will!.....
And I have seen and celebrate in you
The patient, tender truth and trust and care,
The soul's perfection breathing into life
Thro' love's obscure and elemental ways.....

The WOMAN

You love me! I am she! I am the quest,
I am the goal! — You love me!

The POET

I have learned
How, in the last fulfilment of the spirit,
There is a nobler end for life than love,
There is a nobler end for love than you!

The WOMAN

You have not well beheld me, who I am, —
The Stranger Woman, even the truth of dreams,
Splendid and strong and secret.....

The POET

Fairer still
Is the celestial bride, and statelier!.....
I have so greatly loved you that my love

Is grown out of its childhood, which you are,
To more than you can welcome — more than all
Your love and you can freely welcome home!
I am alone and silent after all;
For none receive me now, none love me now.....
Time was when you received me, when your heart
Was radiant and a refuge to me!—then
I uttered and was heard! — and I devised
To set the sunset-coloured gem of song
Upon your brows, to make your raiment of
The unquiet silver of calm, moonlit seas,
To give you sandals hued like flowers, and fill
Your eyes with daybreak, and transfuse your hair
With forest-twilights when the leaves are young
And it is morning!.....Then I said the new,
The utmost things, and all things of you; kissed
The wine-cup and your lips — straitly to feel
The sacred frenzy shake this heart that bears
The sacred flame, until I sang to you
The wonder-song of the primeval earth —
How Eros was first-born of all the Gods,
And first made Chaos pregnant of the world.
O there was that to rouse me in a woman! —
The beauty that is wanton as life is;
The candour that is crystal-clear as stars;
The love that has no other end but life,
The life that has no other end but love;
And all she is not, and the secrecy

She is, — and life's lost wisdom, pure of thought,
Which rises in her from what sunless springs!..
But now the ecstasies of thought advance
The torch beyond the precincts of your love,
Beyond the human pale of your dominion.

The WOMAN

So does life weary when its youth is spent —
And you count weariness a kind of wisdom!
O you are wise — in words! You are a poet!
The cheat is not too plain. Yet one discerns
How you are chafed and sharpened with desire!
The thrill strikes thro' — and you make poems of it,
Since there 's imagination left at least
To prove us how we are not respectable
And give to lust a lyric rapture: — Yes!
Tamed tho' he be, the animal will sing!

The POET

The animal will sing and drink and lust
And lie with you and love you — as a beast
Can love!.....for these and all hilarities
Of the hot blood are still and anciently
The same — they share their excellence with you!
It is alone the spirit which is chaste;
Which is austere and high; which is not eased
By all old pious and pleasurable things;
Which is athirst for news! — and in the search

Is ventured out of your horizons, far
Gone past you and beyond you, to return
No more..... whether the quest prove real or vain!
I guess myself is more than you suppose,
And excellent even beyond my dreams! —
Who shall instruct me further what I am
And shame my aspiration by their own?
Not you, indeed! I know your message to me.
You tell me nothing: for it is not I,
The lyric voice, the florid animal,
The lover, who is yours — as he must be
Who asks neither advancement nor the news!

The WOMAN

What are you more than sense and sentiment,
Like other men? I have known men enough! —
And many men your betters, and some men
Strained to a singular high attitude
Like yours, — and I have found where lust was laired
In all of them! You leave me undeceived:
The brute nurses his passions at your breast,
And at the heart of your humanity
There is the weak, wild longing of all men
Merely for love and life's companioned joys
And the mild fruit of happiness.

The POET

Not I
Am minded any more for facile things.

FIRST SCENE

For the indwelling God stirs in his sleep
Within me, seeing in dreams the early light
Of dawn blur the blind casement of his room.....

The WOMAN

Poor windy man, so grandly, with God's name,
Mystic and eloquent! O you are desolate
As a dead mind! I may not well believe
Laughter stirs nowhere in you — as in me
It leaps to shatter down your dreams.....

The POET

Of all
Sad things I least can laugh with you. Despise,
Pity me as you will, yet so it is:
I have not any sense of humour in me!
I was not once so naked to the truth,
So daring and defenceless; I was keen-
Sighted to see the humour of the thing
And none outlaughed me! — but at last I felt
Something more terrible than ridicule
Strangely and stern as justice in myself!
Then your alert and cherished humour-sense
Sickened and all died out in me, died utterly
Away..... and left me with an abject smile,
Which, like a threadbare cloak, can scarce afford
Decent concealment to me from the world, —
And something that still serves for laughter when

The wine is in me!..... But my secret is
That I am serious! You will think me mad!
But there have lightened to my inward eye
Spacious and radiant serenities
Wherein there is a voice calling me on!.....
My heart is shaken with the power of it!
Before my citadel it sounds a challenge
To wake the audacious virtues of the soul,
Which are themselves their own sole arbiter! —
Therefore I can no longer laugh with you.
I am too tensely nerved with expectation
Still to discern and celebrate the joke,
And sort my mood with yours.

A moment's pause.

And so all's said,
And I will leave you with your life, your love,
Your laughter — which I neither serve nor share.

Night has fallen. The POET pauses a moment and then starts to go. The WOMAN rises, suddenly and prepares to follow him.

The WOMAN

It shall not be — I will not leave you now.

A moment's silence while the POET looks at her intently.

The POET

Why do you follow me?

FIRST SCENE

The WOMAN

I have no light.

The POET

And have I any you are witness of? —
You know not what I am nor where I go.

The WOMAN

I have discerned that you are something more
Than other men, to me. You give my life
Serious, at last, and strange significance.
And there is latent in your words to me
Expression of supreme and secret things,
Phrases of song that bring a high, swift sense
Of flight and of adventure to the soul!
And what I have received of other men
You give me not — the love, the lust, the gold,
Which are a woman's price to the whole world.
O, I am curious of the fellowship
Of one who will not love me lest he lose
The marriage-kiss of the celestial bride, —
Lest being my master he is not his own,
And gaining me he lose himself thereby.
Therefore I will not leave you — for a little.....
It may be I shall one day touch the term
And find the worth of words, as now I am
Not curious of love nor eager any more.
Then I shall leave you.....and go on with life,
Satiated anew and hungry as of old!

The POET

Hungry ? — for news ! for news !.....You know it too,
The hunger and the thirst that drive us on,
As once the gad-fly drove across the world
The paranymph of God, delirious Io ?
You know the hunger ?— then we'll go together,
Whither we cannot tell, nor to what end !

End of the First Scene.

SECOND SCENE

A later hour of the same night as in the first scene. A feast in the palace of CREON.

About the feast-table are CREON, HERAKLES, AMPHITRYON, ALCMENA, MEGARA, IOLAUS, and other men and women of noble Theban families. A HERALD stands behind the King's chair. The feast is served by slaves and the door guarded by soldiers.

SECOND SCENE

CREON

to the HERALD

The feast is ended. Call for silence!

The HERALD

Silence!

Silence! The King will speak!

There is silence. Then is heard a murmur as of a great throng outside the palace. A moment's pause.

CREON

Hearken!.....To-night
There is a rumour in my porticoes
Of multitudes. It is my people. I
Have called them, and this hour would straitly speak
With them and you. I have not lightly caused
Assemblage of yourselves and all the sons
Of Cadmus, for with news of great concern
To all my people am I charged to-night.

To the guards

Therefore set open wide the doors and bid

HERAKLES

My Thebans enter! I have words to say
And deeds to do that must not longer wait.

The doors are thrown open and the people enter without confusion. Gradually the entire hall is completely filled. When they are all entered and silence is reëstablished,

CREON

without rising; in an even, clear, quiet voice

Children of Cadmus — Thebans — Citizens —
My people!—Hear me for your own concern!
And rest assured I treat to-night with you
No less a matter than the commonwealth.
Yet I beseech you to be patient with me
Also for some small business of my own —
Some phrases of a life's apology
That I've matured with life itself for you,
And now at last have ordered and prepared —
Briefly, at least, and cheerfully!— to suit
Your understanding—and my own as well!

A moment's pause.

I am your King; and I am old—and wise!
For wisdom—when the latter end of life
Becomes indeed a luminous and large
Tranquillity, as of some afternoon
Of Autumn and calm weather by the sea—
Inures at last — after so many years! .....
At least there is a fine unfettered sense
Of liberality which leads me on

SECOND SCENE

To say that I am wise — and you will judge
And disapprove me if you must! You may
Believe me that I know what must be done
While there is hope and Fortune's face is toward;—
And I can now afford your censure! Yes,
I can afford at last expensive things
Which cost a man the kingdoms of the world
And all their glory! I have lived my life;
And there is nothing now can make it worth
My while to shirk by any cant or creed,
Enthusiasm or expectancy,
Silence or sentiment, the free, extreme
Analysis, the unrelenting, clear,
Calm vision of a disenchanted mind.
You cannot bribe me now by any threat
Of ruin to my life's high edifice,
Or any dazzled prospect of ambition —
Hope or desire that it may one day grow
Statelier and all my dreams come true of it!—
To keep the old, pathetic, pitiable
Conspiracy of silence and pretence
That barely saves the faith on which you build!
I know that you must build while there is hope
Of profit, while the Bride is beautiful,
While Fortune's prize, in whatsoever coin
The world receives, inflames you to the task;
And while you build you cannot help but say
Your architecture is the noblest art —

The only art that life can labour at!
You see the torch of life held high and bright
Over my disillusion, and your hearts
Are sad for me—but I rejoice with you!
For I have built — and care not very much
What happens! I am patient of all fools
Who leave the why unasked; and I am mild
With knaves, who teach the bawdy, blatant beast
Pious and pleasant ways, — for I am old
And unimpassioned and contemplative.
I think, despite these sceptical strange words,
You will respect me, — for I am your King,
And I have proved myself among you all
An architect. Therefore you will not say,
"This is the voice of failure!"—yet I know
That you will find some other things to say
Not half so true! For when a man is old,
He knows, at least, how utterly himself
Has failed! But say what things of me you will—
And be assured I sympathize! Indeed,
A voice like mine is no-wise terrible,
As might be the tremendous voice of truth,
Should it find speech that you could understand!
Yet it may vex and dreadfully distress
Reflective men — if such indeed there be
Among you all — and therefore be assured
I sympathize!

A moment's pause.

SECOND SCENE

And so I give you thanks.....
And take my leave. I think you almost guess
The public business which is your concern—
And mine, since I concern the state and you.
Briefly 't is mete that I advise you of it:
I am your King—and will be so no more!
Take leave of me, my people! for at last
I have divined a man more apt than I
To wage your wars and guide your policies.—

A moment's pause. The King rises. All those seated at table follow his example.

To him, Children of Cadmus, O my people,
I yield your government, as I bequeath,
When I am dead, my crown and realm to him!
His praise is in your hearts; and by my will,
And with your leave and loving welcome, he
Shall be your Lord and govern in my place,
Who slew Erginus and delivered Thebes—
My grandsons' father and in love my son—
Herakles!

The HERALD

Hail! All hail to Herakles!

A storm of enthusiasm breaks out among the people. When it has subsided and quiet is restored, all eyes turn to HERAKLES. A moment of silence. Then he begins to speak, finding his words with excitement and difficulty.

HERAKLES

Children of Cadmus! — You have heard the King —
You know his will — but mine you shall not know
Till all is known and there is Justice in me!.....
Justice—and Truth!..... Nothing is yet resolved —
Nothing!..... And who can tell what Truth shall be?
The adventurer departs; the tidal drift
Clutches his keel; his eyes are dazed and dark;
Strange are his dreams; — and the discovery
Is far!.....But should I find myself, be sure
That I will be a guide unto you all!.....

A moment's pause.

I'll say no more!—Nothing is yet resolved.....

A moment of silence. At last the people applaud. Then, at a sign from the King, the doors are again thrown open and the citizens pass out. The King remains standing after they are gone. MEGARA, ALCMENA, AMPHITRYON, IOLAUS and the other guests at the feast surround HERAKLES, pouring forth congratulations and applause. HERAKLES, deeply moved, withdraws violently from the embraces of his family and the acclamations of his friends and, turning toward the King, breaks silence with profound passion.

HERAKLES

Is this your wisdom, Sire? and is it wise,
Lightly, and thus with calm complacency,

Now to believe that I, that Herakles
Should hold himself so cheaply as your price?
How have you come to think me, whom you love
And praise, so vain a thing and spiritless,
That I, like any rash, rapacious man,
Should seize this brief preferment and renown
And block with brilliant insufficiencies
The fair-way of ambition? — By the Gods,
How pitiable a thing is man's regard!
Since you, who count yourself matured in truth,
Can guess no nobler destiny for man
Than all his life to be as you have been,
Public and proud, constrained and crafty-wise,
As fortune served and chance was bountiful:—
Himself, the while, illiberal and unknown,
Captive and undelivered and deceived!

Turning to the others

And you! I marvel who it is you name,
With tears and praise and passion, Herakles!
By God! What gives you leave to think of me
So meanly, and rejoice to see me sold
Like any common man for a small thing?
Have I not loved you all, incessantly
Loved you and lived with you?—yet in despite
Of all love's witness and the test of time
You dare to hold me in so little honour
That you have thought me apt to be content

HERAKLES

In these safe human mediocrities—
That you have deemed my hope so temperate,
For what I am, as fortune and renown
Or all the world's casual supremacies!
For my whole life long, with my whole heart's love,
I have been with you—and you have not known me!

ALCMENA

What ails you, child?.....My child! I love you, know
you—
You are my son!

HERAKLES

My self is yet unborn,
Which was not when your womb conceived and bore!

AMPHITRYON

What rage is this? Implore the King's forgiveness!
Pray to the Gods who have shown favour to you!

HERAKLES

turning to the King

Sire, I will not serve the Gods or you!
Sire, I will not rule by grace of God
Or by your grace! I will be Lord of none,
And thus unto myself be Lord and Law!—

No longer speaking directly to the King

You think to bribe and browbeat Herakles,

Force his desire and cheat his hope:—at last
Learn from my lips that I will not be less
In hope or longing than a man must be!
I, with the soul's immortal thirst to slake,
How shall I down into the shallow stream
Where beasts and many men have drunk together
And left foul waters strangled in their course?
Nay, by this cup I am not comforted,
I am not stayed!—Rather, I swear to you
Thirst shall consume me unappeased until
I fill my pitcher at the living source,
The secret, spiritual springs that rise,
Radiant and crystalline in the deep light,
Far on the utmost heights unvisited!
You know me not—and scarce have I begun
To know myself! Yet this at least I know:
The life-lust and the florid animal
Which laughs and longs, is pleasured and distressed—
The heart that feels and feigns, that faints and dreams,
That sorrows and is glad—the facile brain
That schemes and lies and is alert to seize
Success and is ambitious of no more
Than serviceable ingenuity
Can aptly compass—that supremely serves
To methodize the waste of the world's work
To profitable order and endow
Life's labour with a seeming worth and end—
These are not I!

CREON

Your pardon! — and be sure
I have no angered heart nor outraged pride
To vex you with!—I pray you answer me
One idle question: — after all, what else
Is there of you save life and heart and brain?
You are what feels and thinks and is. What else
Is Herakles? — are you?

HERAKLES

I am what knows!
I am myself, that knows—and shall be known!.....

End of the Second Scene.

THIRD SCENE

Later of the same night as in the first two scenes. It is a clear, calm night of moon and stars. A public street near the city wall. At regular intervals the wall is rendered accessible by flights of narrow stone steps. The inner face of the wall is in a deep shadow which stretches out almost to the street.

HERAKLES *appears, emerging from the shadow, as he climbs the nearest flight of steps. He reaches the top of the wall and pauses a moment in silence.*

THIRD SCENE

HERAKLES

I know them now.....but me they shall not know,
Even at last! My youth was spent with them;
They were my most familiar and my friends —
My lovers and the lights of welcome to me.....
Yet they discerned me not, they knew not me!.....
And never shall they know what I become!
Death is between us now: my youth is dead,
And I am dying!.....and I shall be reborn
Beyond their understanding and their love.....
Even now I was a very stranger to them!
How shall it be when all myself has been
Is passed away and I am born again?.....
I dare not yet believe how utterly
I shall be loveless then — even when love is
A better thing to give, and, to receive,
A more exalted thing!.....Then I shall know,
And be unknown; I shall be friendless then
However I am heart-sick and alone! —
O tender twilights of the days gone by,
Peopled with those we loved and leave behind! —
O secret, great departures, shared by none,
Cheered by no friendly voices from the shore,
No lamps set seaward for the ship's return! —

HERAKLES

O irremediable solitude
Of him who sails, adrift and harbourless,
Far out into the distance and the dawn! —
Speak to my heart — when shall my lover come?
Where is my friend? and how shall I be known?
And who shall know me?.....When the Child is born,
The desolate immortal Child, I know
That in the night of his tremendous birth,
And in the dreadful solitude, he wails
And wonders and is no-wise comforted!
Shall none receive the Child? Am I at once
The knower and the known? Is there no light
From soul to soul, no love from heart to heart
Can span the abyss and flame across the cold,
Dark, dreadful spaces of my isolation?.....
I need assurance, now since love has failed
So far, and life has so far failed to prove
Myself or make me manifest to men.
Who shall assure me and bear witness to me?
Whence shall the signal — as from star to star
Rings the clear cry of the celestial choir —
Sound thro' the tragic taciturnities
Of solitude, to me?.....to me at last! —
Love to the Lover, welcome to the Friend,
Raptures of recognition to the Lord!.....

HERAKLES pauses a moment; then turns and slowly goes back down the steps by which he ascended. As he descends he becomes gradually engulfed in the deep shadow. Before he reaches the ground, the POET and the WOMAN appear ascending to the wall by another flight of steps, some distance away. They reach the top and pause a moment gazing over the landscape. When at last they begin to speak, the sound of their voices causes HERAKLES to stop; and he continues to stand attentive and stirless in the shadow of the wall.

The POET

.....Where is Endymion? The moon replies,
Hence is my lover!.....and the heart cries, Hence!.....
And hence the soul discerns the perfect friend!.....
They lure us hence, the patient hills and fields;
The streams persuade us hence — hence to the sea,
Where as of old the mythos of the life
Of man enacts its endless destiny,
And vast horizons indicate the soul!.....
Hence is the furtherance of hope —

The WOMAN

The song
You lately sang cries to the spirit, Hence!
Sing me the song again, for I would learn
The words and have it in my heart alway.

The POET

I made it on a day of happiness,
And I am glad to-night — of life, and you.

HERAKLES

He sings.

He is on the road before us, who is Lord and Life and Lover,
He is forward in the fair-way, he is secret, swift and far;
And our eyes shall wake to find him and our hungry hearts discover,
As he leads us, where we follow; as he loves us, what we are!

Where the winds are shouting seaward, where the sea is streaming onward,
Where the Voice calls down to find us, fearless on the starlit way,
We who watch shall make the land-fall as the ship drives shoreward, sunward,
Where the mountains rise resplendent, rose-wreathed in the dawn of day!

There his heart shall be our father-house, his arms receive and hold us; —
As he knows us we are equal; as he trusts us we are free!
We shall learn surpassing secrets that no lips but his have told us,
We shall find in his embrace ourselves transformed to more than we!

And thereafter in his house shall he alone be Lord and
Master;
Life shall yield to his dominion; they shall serve who
once were proud;
We shall go with him together up the pathway fast and
faster;
We shall see the stars surround us as his eyes dissolve
the cloud!

We shall see the skies stand open; we shall hear the
stars in chorus;
From the shining peaks of thought his voice shall
answer, pure and high;
And the spacious gates of light shall stand asunder full
before us;
And, as all alone we enter, we shall know the Lord
is I!

The WOMAN

How mystic, mad and possible it seems,
How like a clearance of life's tangled skein,
To dream, to say, to sing, "I am the Lord!"
Poet! you know me better than myself.....

The POET

My poems are made of more than all I know.....

A moment of silence.

The WOMAN

Shall we go farther on? — no matter where,
So we go on.....

The POET

How the heart melts with song!.....
How the brain reels in the storm-wind of thought!.....
Come, let us go! The light is there.....

The POET and the WOMAN turn and go down the wall, away from the spot where HERAKLES is standing. The two figures seem to disappear in the distance.

HERAKLES

emerging from the shadow into the moonlit street

The light!—
There where my dreams discern an excellence
Unrealized, which I am—whither I go!.....
I have but matched the beast with other beasts,
The man with other men; and when my strength,
Impatient and unused, challenged me on,
I have but guessed that haply, with the Gods
At strife, God was within me, to defy
Their curse and prove their equal and prevail!
Now let me learn to say, I am the Lord!
Since in the forward vistas of my hope,
There is the Lord, the Saviour — there am I!
For thus I am assured my end is not
Where the world ends and humble hopes go home;
Where men are crowned and beasts are satiated!—

THIRD SCENE

Too well I know that I contain them all —
The serpent, wolf and jackal, ape and cur,
Lion and hog: — of old the beasts are laired
In life's primeval wilderness, the dark,
Trackless and devil-haunted waste within me!.....
Yet, in the mind's rapt outlook, I discern
That in the jungle is the Householder,
Whose patient labour has made room and home
And let the light into his dwelling-place!
Now, while he sleeps, it may be, in his stead
Garrulous ghosts and fauns infest the gloom
And in his name accomplish shameful deeds,
Shallow and eloquent sincerities,
Profession of all faiths that falsify,
And threadbare fashions of a masquerade —
While from the teeming dark they snarl and whine,
Chatter and roar and laugh, gibber and grin
With greedy eyes and fangs — the beasts, the beasts
Who harbour where his realm is unreclaimed!.....
Yet I believe he shall not sleep alway!
Nay, he shall wake and witness — and suspect
Himself is otherwise than all of these!.....
O he shall stake his life upon that vision!
And he shall wonderfully at last contrive
To bring the outlawed beasts into dominion
And hold them captive — having levelled down
The dark recesses where they crouched untamed!
He shall dispel the spectres, and return

HERAKLES

The jungle to a fruitful harvest-field! —
And then—O then, after the victory,
He shall go forth in power and look abroad
Over the spacious acres of the soul,
All drowned in azure and tranquillity,
Where, all bearing his harness and subdued,
The mighty beasts labour and drive afar
The ploughshare of his will, and spread the seed,
And reap the harvest — and proclaim the Lord
In word and deed, and celebrate the Lord!.....
Then shall he know the Lord is I! and feel
That ecstasy of knowledge which is truth,
Which is religion, which is self and soul!.....

The voice of IOLAUS
calling in the near distance

Answer me, Lord!.....Where art thou?.....Speak to me!.....

IOLAUS appears.

Lord, is it thou?.....

HERAKLES

He said — the Lord is I!

End of the Third Scene.

FOURTH SCENE

Toward midnight of the same night as in the first three scenes. Street before the house of HERAKLES.

MEGARA and the THREE SONS OF HERAKLES are in the house.

FOURTH SCENE

The voice of MEGARA
low and sweet from within the house

The rose-wreathed lattice opens wide,
Beyond, the night is calm and deep;—
My little doves lie fast asleep
Like lilies fallen side by side.

They laid them down at evening;
Their eyes were clear as moonlit dew;
Across their brows the sunset threw
The golden shadow of its wing.

HERAKLES and IOLAUS enter slowly. They pause and listen.

They kissed my face, with tender words;
Their eyelids closed as flowers close;
In dreamless, motionless repose
They fell asleep like tired birds.

HERAKLES

Iolaus.....

IOLAUS

Lord?

HERAKLES

So Pyrrha in the dark
Sang to the children of Deukalion.....
So long as there is life it shall not cease,
It shall not change, this tender lullaby,
This ancient minstrelsy of motherhood.
Wherever there is human happiness
Or human grief or life's immortal will,
The inviolate serenities of night
Shall hear the woman singing to her sons,
Her little doves — my children, Iolaus!
Who shall be men, as they shall wake from sleep,
Radiant in the morning, and the might
Of manhood!.....

The voice of MEGARA
as before

My children sleep, whose lives fulfil
The soul's tranquillity and trust;
While clothed in life's immortal dust
The patient earth lies dark and still.

No rumour rises from the street;
The stars in silence dawn and die;
The moon goes up the violet sky
And treads the sea with silver feet;

And calm as inward joy, and deep,
Moonlight and starlight flood the room

FOURTH SCENE

Where close beside me in the gloom
Softly my little children sleep.

All night they lie against my breast
And sleep, whose dream of life begins:
Before the time of strife and sins,
Of tears and truth, they take their rest.

HERAKLES

.....They take their rest!.....Iolaus! Iolaus!
What of the soul? Can you not feel — as I
To-night bore witness to you all — that we,
Who seem to wake in the large light of life
So sensibly, in pure reality
Lie in the shadow of sleep, lie prone and still
On the parental breast of life like children,
And take our rest?.....

IOLAUS

Yet we have witness, Lord,
Who have so wrought in the substantial world, —
Yet we have witness that we wake indeed:
Is not Erginus slain, Orchomenos
Razed and enslaved, and Herakles —

HERAKLES

Enough! —
Not by the world's coarse manifest I am!
To me no voice but mine can testify:

HERAKLES

The violence and the glare of deeds and things
Report me in no wise: — myself alone
Proves and reveals myself: no other sign
Is there at all of me save only I!
Have I not ceaselessly been here and there,
Come hither and gone hence, ambitiously
And humanly lived out my works and days?
Have I not gone abroad seeking the soul
In vast and various venture, and returned
Weary and without wisdom after all?
When have I known myself, who know the world?
When have I felt, in trial or victory,
The choir, the torch, the festival of truth
Gladden the soul's inviolate dwelling-place?.....
Now am I no more eager of many things;
Neither am I much curious of proof,
Save as some still conviction, secretly
Wakes in the inmost mind and justifies
New lights, new values, new coherencies,
New strengths and virtues up the endless scale.
For well I know how anciently and long
The massive Sphinx has stood as now it stands,
A veiled, portentous shape of shadow and silence,
Against the nightfall in the mind's dark highway;
And well I know that, anciently as now,
To the inscrutable mystery of being
There is no voice shall answer save the clear
Silences singing in the awakened soul!.....

FOURTH SCENE

IOLAUS

There is no voice shall answer!.....Is there more
Of man's inheritance than all we know?
Are we not merely men who labour and live
In the plain light, in the gross world; who rest
By night; who fall asleep at last in death;
Who feel, invincibly, darkly over us,
The harsh dominion of the inconstant Gods?

HERAKLES

Nay! We are adepts of a mystery!.....
The secret is at hand—how shall we sleep?
We are as men in awful expectation
Before the threshold of a sanctuary,—
Whose eyes grow sometimes clear in the long vigil,
Whose hearts grow sometimes mild, till they discern
The glamour of a glory on the veil,
The murmur of a music thro' the portal—
The secret, incommunicable signs
Of the God's radiant presence in his house!

The voice of MEGARA
as before

My little doves, the nest is warm—
Lie close! the dawn shall come too soon.
Sleep, in the quiet of the moon!
Sleep, in the hollow of my arm!

HERAKLES

For yesterday is all we are,
    To-morrow all we yet shall be;
    The end is where no eye can see.....
We only know the way is far!

We only know men grow and grieve
    And die.....And death is strange and sore!
    O sleep, my darlings, sleep!—before
The time returns to wake — to live!

A moment of silence.

HERAKLES

The ancient, patient, perfect love of women!.....
The service and the sacrifice of life
To life!.....But to what end of life?.....Her voice
Is clear and quiet as moonlit well-water
In a vessel of shining silver.....This is home!

A moment of silence.

IOLAUS

Let us enter, Lord.

HERAKLES

I shall not sleep to-night.
I know not how it is, there is within me
To-night a stern, unquiet intensity,
The strangeness of a secret unrevealed —
Almost, it seems, a fear of what I am!.....
I am as some itinerant by night,

Ignorant of his purpose and his path,
Curious of both, vigilant, fearful, fain,
Sleepless and sightless till the dawn is there!.....
I shall not stay or sleep. No more to me
The rash and resolute activities
Of manhood sound to-night their martial challenge
Into the bright arena of the world.
I am this hour inviolably alone,
And like a stranger in my solitude.....
A glitter of far lights is in my brain,
And in my heart something that is not hope,
And in my life a hushed suspense.....To-night,
Beyond the threshold and the fire-light,
Beyond the brief, familiar place of being,
Held by the narrow candle-flame of life
Against the invasive, dark, immense unknown,
I am abroad!.....The heart's unrest is nameless
And absolute the mind's uncertainties!
Ask me not whither, where or why I go:
The spacious night surrounds me, and my spirit
Ranges magnificently unappeased!.....

IOLAUS

Why must you go abroad seeking a dream
When here at home all is so bountiful?
Here the King's daughter croons your sons asleep;
Here Creon has given over to your hands
His kingship by your mighty hands secured;

Here in all Greece your name is glorious,
Your deeds extolled, your worth proclaimed in praise;—
Here your estate is grown so high and splendid
That hardly can the range of man's ambition
Compass a nobler destiny than yours!

HERAKLES

So is the range of man's ambition brief
And scanted of his true divinity!

IOLAUS

Why is your speech so strange to-night?

HERAKLES

'T is I
Am strange!.....And now I think my heart would break
To hear her sing again, to feel once more
The tenderness and the tranquillity
And sweetness of her love, — the delicate
Freshness of life's warm wonder in my house.
Come, let us go! — I shall not rest to-night.

IOLAUS

Where shall I follow, since you will not sleep?

HERAKLES

Let us go down into the human city,
Iolaus, where men and women with their sins

FOURTH SCENE

Stray in the festive street; where harp-players
And harlots and young men sit in the taverns,
And feel, all night until the daybreak stands
Pale and relentless in the waking world,
Life's wanton weed grow rankly in their souls!
Let us go down into the human city
And see how men and women love and live,
Whose feet go forward to the sepulchre,
Whose hearts are sick with tender syllables
Unspoken, and desires unsatisfied,
And liberalities no heart receives.....
Let us go down! — perchance they wait us there,
The meaning and the sign! — let us go down!

End of the Fourth Scene.

FIFTH SCENE

Before dawn of the next day. A street before a tavern. At intervals is heard the sound of music and voices and occasional bursts of laughter from within.

HERAKLES and IOLAUS enter.

FIFTH SCENE

IOLAUS

Now nothing more is left to seek or see.
Let us return. We have been long abroad;
We have been up and down the sleepless city
And far afield from where is happiness.....
Let us return.

HERAKLES

Here's still a last, least place
Where laughter is, where there is light and wine
And song.....

IOLAUS

And this is last, of all: beyond,
The lampless thoroughfare goes far away
Into the darkness, past the city wall.
Here we are come to the road's end. The earth
Lies out beyond, spacious and tranquil, where
The moonlight, like the nimbus that surrounds
A sage in meditation, quietly
And vastly and serenely luminous,
Lies, pale as dreams are pale, over the world!.....

Laughter is heard within the tavern. Then there is a moment of silence.

HERAKLES

Hark!.....How serene is silence!.....How austere!.....
How spacious!.....And how small and sad a thing
Is laughter — and how sometimes terrible!.....
There is no rumour save the sound of mirth
When souls are lost!.....I know not how it seems
To you, but I believe the Minotaur
Kept out of sight and sound like a good fellow,
And there was laughter in the labyrinth,
And it was pleasant for them who were lost —
Lost without hope, nor any vision of hope,
Nor any faith to vex them with ambition!
Hark!.....How they laugh and sing and take no
heed,
The boys, the panders, and the singing-women,
The harlot and her ruffian! — And ourselves,
Iolaus, ourselves, who keep so delicate,
Who live so chaste and private — who are we,
Who fill with rumour as of a festival
The public precincts of the House of Life? —
Who vex the soul with gilt caparisons
And go in power and pride and policy,
Panders to profit and the world's applause,
About the brilliant business of the world?
Are we not of this ribald company,
These toilers for the selfsame prize as we,
Only of less profession and renown —
These merrymakers in the labyrinth,

FIFTH SCENE

Who singing sit beside the sallow tapers,
Derelict, dispossessed, delinquent, — dead?
Why so we are, by God! — king, soldier, priest,
Cut-purse and prostitute — in fact the same
Poor men and women, all of us — so kin,
So far adrift, so dark, so solitary!.....
Then let's within and claim our fellowship!
They are of us — and they shall not be denied!

IOLAUS

Nay, we have seen to-night too much of this.
Let us return! The street and the night end.
Let us return — my heart is sick for home!.....

HERAKLES

O we are very far from where is home
To that within us which is comfortless —
The heart that is not patient of our thrift;
The soul that is not pleasured as we are
In safe, substantial mediocrity!
To-night, in street and tavern, anxiously,
Like children fatherless and dispossessed,
We were come out to seek our heritage;
We were come out to seek for more than all
Our lives have variously informed us of,
And more than all we know! — What rest is there,
Or where shall we go home, who have not found
Ourselves or what is ours? Whither away

And in what casement stands the lamp for us
Who drift as might a helmless derelict,
Errant with wind and tide over dark seas?
This shall we hardly learn at last to know;
And hardly shall our hearts receive the sign,
Our eyes find fire along the forward way,
Till that reprieve of freedom, peace and power
When we have saved the grain and strawed the chaff
With a most jealous fan throughout the ripe
Acreage of the spirit's harvest-field!.....
Truly I am not now as once I was,
Replete, exultant, proved, resistless, proud,
When all the Sons of Cadmus hailed me victor!
Rather my joy is quelled of all my deeds;
For worth is of myself, and I have none.....
Yet do they rate me by no means, whose choice
And crown proclaim me Lord! It well may be
You doubt me. True, I know not what it means—
And all is doubt!.....Yet there is born within me
To-night a sense of outcast solitude,
The darkness of a flame-rent thunder-cloud,
And peril and devastation in my brain,—
While in my heart, like devious, distant fire,
The thread of hope leads thro' the labyrinth!.....
What is the whole of life—when dreams come true;
When faith is realized; when the mind unlocks
The treasure-house of truth; when, loosed and winged,
Ambition ceases of itself to be

So gross, so measured, so commensurate
With possible and perishable things?.....

The voice of the WOMAN
singing in the tavern

I know not why we drink and feast
Unless it be to make us laugh,
Who waste the grain and store the chaff,
Who starve the God and glut the beast!

Yet know I not how wine can make,
Of all sad things, a woman smile;
For what is wine to so beguile
The heart that bleeds and will not break?

I know but this — we cannot bear
The truth that laughter hides so well!.....
And all the damned dead souls in Hell
Scream with eternal laughter there!

A rumour of voices in the tavern.

IOLAUS

Poor wanton wretch! — God pity her!

HERAKLES

Not so!
Bravely she sings her heart out, and in tune,
And strictly to the measure of its truth.

She knows the cost of some things — and their worth!
And briefly she has made a song of how
Her life is bankrupt for some scraps of tinsel.
No God is wise enough to pity her,
Nor sad enough! Her tragedy is yours
And mine; — O verily this alone is all
Life's tragedy, that in the strict account
Of truth we find — whose lives were cheaply sold
At the world's price in chaplet, coin or crown —
Such meagre profit, such tremendous loss!
And be assured it is not pitiable
To sing one's heart out, as she sings, of it:
Bravely, and not too sadly — and in tune!

The rumour of voices is renewed in the tavern. Then silence. A pause.

The voice of the POET
singing in the tavern

I know not what it is appears
To us so worth the tragic task: —
I know beneath his ribald masque
Man's sightless face is grey with tears!

I know not why it is we dread
To lie in death's embrace, alone: —
I know that he receives a stone
Who asks with all his love for bread!

FIFTH SCENE

I know not how, I know not why
 We save the hope that naught fulfils: —
 I know that life constrains and kills
The dying soul that will not die!.....

The rumour of voices breaks out in the tavern, louder than before.

HERAKLES

Hearken!.....and hear the voice of human woe,
Crying aloud and crude and comfortless!
Hark, from the cheated and distempered mind,
This harsh and ancient outburst of despair
Proclaim we are all perdurable men
And perjured souls and hearts that still conserve
A pitiable efficiency of pain!
Then question of yourself, and you shall find
His voice is mine and yours — if we could sing!
In each of us the serpent of despair
Sleeps — or is roused and strikes his poisoned fangs
Deep in the heart and brain, till one must die,
The serpent or the soul, — unless we charm
Serpent and soul with song! For song alone
Makes tolerable to us the acrid lees,
When time and truth have trod life's wine-press out,
Which, undiluted, in thought's crystal cup,
Are of too cogent anguish to the soul.

He charms who is not strong enough to slay!
He sings who is not brave enough to know,
And in himself feel truth exemplified!
Thus, I believe, the tragic poet sings
Because he fails to do a better thing:
Up from the ruins of his failure starts
The phœnix-bird of song: — he knows the while
How far aloft God's eagle eyes the sun!.....
Had we the will, the strength, the hardihood
To let the light inform us utterly,
And so transfuse and interchange with all
Gross elements that we were born again,
Perfect and true; — had we the stern resolve
And power and passion of our sacred cause
To bear the pangs of childbirth to the end,
And die to live; — in such comparison
What were a life's magnificence of song?.....
God is within the soul — and who has been
A little toward Him, sings! There is no more
To do for one who leaves the best undone.....
The poet wakes, indeed, — but merely sings!
Yet therefore is he more than other men;
For they come hardly into wakefulness,
And briefly, and in terror and great pain,
Soon to relapse, latent and lost in sleep.....
Are we not all, in silence and alone,
Sepulchred living under dreams and dust?.....
And if at last we dreadfully revive,

FIFTH SCENE

Straitened and gagged in death's caparisons,
Within the unspeakable solitude and dense
Silence and brutal blackness of the grave,
'T is but to glimpse the shining star of hope
With false persuasion of transcendent joy —
And then, as faith's uplifted face dislimns,
To die immobile in the narrow night,
Our hearts constricted with a frenzied fear
Of death's deceit, — with life's supreme appeal!
The poet sings — and lives! And I believe,
Should one audacious rebel — even the soul's
Champion — who was not eased with poems, essay
His strength against the terror and the tomb,
It might be they should wonderfully yield!
Yea! till he went his way from us, — perchance
To prove the Saviour of us, on his way!

A rumour of voices; then loud applause in the tavern.

A chorus of MEN and WOMEN
singing in the tavern

Dionysos!
God begot thee, woman bore thee,
Dionysos! Now before thee
Dance the Mænads who adore thee,
Who are of thy fellowship!
Every heart is frenzied for thee,
Dionysos! every lip
Glisters with the wine we pour thee,

HERAKLES

Crimson as the sacred stain
When the sacrifice is slain —
Dionysos!

Wild laughter and applause within the tavern.

IOLAUS

Let us go hence, go hence! Behold, the night
Grows pale and passive as a sick man's face
At daybreak as he lies asleep. It dawns.
The livid light comes down the dreadful street
Timidly as a tired vagrant child,
And stands between us here before the tavern,
Naked and shivering in its threadbare dress.

HERAKLES

When shall it be that somewhere in the soul,
Beyond our life's horizons, dark with dreams,
The Child of Light shall rise from sleep and stand
Radiantly in the silent place of peace?.....
When shall it be that he shall venture down
The strange, remote, dark thoroughfares of thought,
And stand with shining feet before the tavern,
Where all night long his servants brawl and feast,
In pale and passionless severity?.....
When shall it be his presence shall eclipse
The flickering, brief, clandestine candle-light
That lust has kindled in the House of Life?.....
When shall he enter by the dolorous door

Of love and faith, where death at last comes in,
And bind the slaves by his resistless will,
Who made his house a place of harlotry
And lies and lamentations and vain deeds
And vice and violence and vociferation?.....
When shall he rise from sleep and go abroad?.....
We know not when — yet surely they shall know
Who keep his vigil! And, within that hour,
At last the slaves' ignoble revelry,
Their spectral humours and hilarities
Shall shudder and be still! — and they shall learn
How little is the Lord indeed from home!
And men shall witness and the Gods shall know
That he is risen — the grave and gracious Lord
Is risen, and on his way! And they shall see
His light go forward, and about his feet
The flowers of spiritual trust and truth
Wake in the silent meadows deep in dusk
Beside the stream-course of the spirit's life!
And they shall hear his voice, serene as stars,
Strengthen to song, like scattered birds who wake
Crying in wet tree-twilights, as with hands
Lustrous and loving he dilates the gloom
With muffled splendour; while, superbly winged,
The deep-eyed virtues of the soul's perfection
Rise like essential perfumes, sweet and strong!.....

The voice of the POET
singing in the tavern

Her eyes were dark as violet;
Her face was white as sunburnt sand.....
Because we could not understand,
Love turned and left us, hand in hand —
Her lips surrendered, red and wet!
I saw in the dishevelled dress
Only her pale, abandoned loveliness!

The voice of the WOMAN
singing in the tavern

He laid his brows against my breast;
He kissed my breast with lips of flame;
His voice made music of my name;
And in the sunless house of shame
Between his arms he held me pressed! —
He knew not what it was to me,
Or what to him, thereafter, love might be!

The voice of the POET
as before

I felt her heart beat hard and high;
I saw her eyes grow blurred and blind; —
There came a mist across my mind.....
Her hair fell round me soft as wind
And lustrous as a moonlit sky.....
For pleasure of her was my breath
Broken, as one who labours near to death!.....

FIFTH SCENE

The voice of the WOMAN
as before

The desolation; the despair;
The hope; the love; the will to be
Spendthrift of the heart's treasury;
The soul's inviolate chastity
Were all of me he could not share!
He asked no more of love than this;
He gave no better than a harlot's kiss!

The voice of the POET
as before

I held her all the dumb night long,
And still at daybreak she was there,
When, groping thro' the dark, dense air,
The dawn's chill fingers touched her bare
Pale body, clear and smooth as song!.....
The stealthy light fell, grey as dust,
Silently in the sordid place of lust!

The voice of the WOMAN
as before

Love cannot enter by the door
Where lust comes fierce and florid in!
They play no game that love can win,
Who stake the outlawed coins of sin,—
Yet love can lose one heart the more!
For truth lies deep beneath the lie;
And Death has digged no grave where souls can die!

The voice of the POET
as before

And silently I went my way;
The heart within me wailed and wept!.....
I would have kissed her as she slept —
And dared not! Like a thief I crept
Scared and alone into the day.....
And Love walked on with bleeding feet,
Heart-sick beside me in the dreadful street!

The voice of the WOMAN
as before

Quenched is the flame in us whereof
Love's sacred lamp is lit; and we
Are captives as damned souls must be;
And hence from Hell shall none go free
Whose lives have lost the key of love! —
Who neither asked nor sought nor knocked,
To them alone Truth's treasure-house is locked!

A confused tumult of voices in the tavern, which gradually subsides until at last there is silence.

IOLAUS

.....On broken heartstrings is their music made!
To hear them laugh and sing I half believe,
As you declare, that laughter broke their hearts.....
And they have fashioned of all shattered things
The phrase of an incomparable grief,

And called it song — which is indeed a cry
Something more strangely sad than any tears.
O come with me to the still house of joy! —
There is a sorrow in the vacant street,
And even the light is like a lamentation.....

He pauses. HERAKLES neither speaks nor stirs.

My heart is sad and strange — let us return!
There is a kind of judgment in the light —
Something austere and chaste and pitiless,
Dealing impartial justice to us all.....
Let us return — for God's sake let us go!
I can no longer bear to hear them sing!

HERAKLES

Hark — there is silence! Hark — and you shall hear,
Vast and inviolate, while they seem to sing,
The inveterate silence of the sepulchre —
Where he is lying inert as dead men lie,
Who is the deathless holy spirit of man —
Massively overwhelm their melody!
There is a sound, a semblance as of song,
A quiver of rhythmic motion in the air.....
But then and still thereafter there is silence,
Strictly distinguished to the inward ear.
Hark — and your soul shall hear it as I do!
They sing not — neither can they sing at all,
Who are as we in bondage to this world!

Their music is a shallow counterfeit,
The unsubstantial echo of a voice;—
Not the phrased splendour of essential song
Rumoured along the surface of the soul's
Deep seas of elemental harmony!.....
Hearken within yourself! Hearken within,
And hear how still, how gaunt and dumb it is!.....
O there is silence, silence in us all!
We are some handfuls of gross clay assembled,
Wherein there is a tremor and a tone,
A pitiable vibration which is song
As men rate song in their discordant lives.....
And far within is silence! — Otherwise,
Otherwise is the full free voice of man,
The one true voice, our own voice! — when there is
No silence by the altar any more;
When there, in strength and in tranquillity,
The hieratic, consecrated soul
Intones its canticle of self-reprieve,
And all its powers and liberties proclaim
The chaunt of the divine awakening!.....

The tavern door opens. A little crowd of men and women stumble noisily into the street. Among them are the POET and the WOMAN. They all pause uncertainly, staring vaguely about them.

A MAN

Here's the damned daylight back again.....

FIFTH SCENE

A HARLOT

God's name,
How cold it is!

The POET

As chill and chaste as death!

A MAN

Let's go back! There's no hospitality
And nothing comfortable in all this world
Save, there within, the wine and candle-light.

The POET

Save drunkenness and dark! — Is there not death?
Poor ghost! Poor tomb-dweller! — Is there not death?

A MAN

I would to God there were death — for all poets!
And silence for all singers, save of some
Small mirthful songs of bawdry and pleasant things.....

A HARLOT

Truth is, Stranger, your songs are keen as pain.

A MAN

His songs are serious — and most damnable!
Wine brings susceptibility — and dawn 's
A desperate hour, when a mere song's grief
May tragically rouse the heart to tears
And vain misgivings.....

HERAKLES

A HARLOT

As for me, I love
To weep when there is music. Give me songs
Of noble sentiment. Tears ease the heart —

A MAN

No tearful wench for me, nor tearful song!
Poets and whining women — damn such fools!
Gay hearts, gay women, gay good-fellowship,
Wine and gay music — so a man is pleased!

The POET

Eyes of the deathless Gods, look down, look down!
Behold this tragic masque of marionettes!.....
And laugh because we weep, and laugh the more
Because we laugh — and lie, and dare not live
In the confession of reality!

A MAN

Damn you, be silent! and deliver us
Of all your tedious solemnities!
Already you have robbed the night of mirth,
And now, despite the wine, nothing is left
But daylight and despondency.....

The WOMAN

In truth
I'll not believe a poet could so far
Vex and subdue your wanton hearts with words.

Are you not men of business and affairs,
Hard men of worldly practice and the world?
And he's — merely a voice! and such a voice
As you shall hardly hear or understand!
Nay, lads, I'll not believe you're out of tune
With laughter for a song's worth of strange words!
Even a poor wench can laugh! — The end of mirth
Comes only when the cheerless heart is cracked
And the frail spark of life flutters and fails!.....

The POET

.....Comes only when we learn there is more hope
Than life can give; more truth than words can say!

A HARLOT

Enough! It's bitter cold here in the dawn,
And I'll no longer wait and freeze and tire
To hear you snarl and curse at one another! —
Let's all to bed!

A MAN

The wench is right — let's go!

They all start off and move, in a straggling group, toward HERAKLES and IOLAUS, whose forms are hardly distinguishable in the grey twilight. Suddenly one of the women halts.

A HARLOT

There are strangers here — yonder!

A MAN

Two men.....

Calling

Who's there?

HERAKLES takes a step forward. A moment of silence.

A MAN

Your pardon!.....If a man may question you,
My Lord, and since we chance to meet — who are you?

A moment of silence. HERAKLES scans the faces before him almost anxiously.

HERAKLES

I am a man who seeks — and has not found;
Who asks — and is not answered; who has knocked —
Yet none has opened to him the secret door.
Do you bring news — and welcome — and the alms?

The WOMAN separates herself from the group and draws nearer to HERAKLES.

A HARLOT

What says he?

A MAN

I can hardly tell.....

A MAN

He seems
In some delusion —

FIFTH SCENE

The POET

Then perhaps he's drunk! —
Are we not all at dawn a little drunk?

The WOMAN

Be still!.....

The POET

What now? Why do you stare and stare?.....
I say his wine has been to many a man
Persuasion of delirious things and words,
And specious dreams of what It's all about.....

The WOMAN

Be still! Look in his eyes!.....

The POET
to HERAKLES

Your pardon, Sir!
The wench has drunk her share —

He turns to the WOMAN. The sight of her thrills and startles him. His whole mood and manner change. He draws close to her and speaks to her alone.

Tell me the news:
Is it the Secret? — Speak!

The WOMAN
speaking as tho' entranced

.....There is within

HERAKLES

His eyes a candid infancy of light—
A birth of splendour — and a mystery!
A vigil — and a voice! — the light that leads,
Convinces and absolves — like sunlight! Far,
Far in his eyes it dawns!..... I seem to see
So far within — so far! His eyes are like
Some sudden window, opening in the night.....
Thence may the soul stare skyward — to the stars!
Look in his eyes, if you have will to see!
All other eyes of men are closed and dark.
Look in his eyes!—O, God's within, I know!
There, in the utmost distance, there is God!.....
There is the light of God, splendid and strange!.....

HERAKLES

with passion

Are you the herald and the messenger?

The POET

Herald of hope and messenger of news!.....

HERAKLES

heedless of all save the WOMAN

Is there indeed light in the window — light
To prove the Lord is in his house and wakes,
Who has slept overlong? You say the light
Is lit, the sign is there to show he wakes
At last — and feels across his solemn brows

The rose-winged wind of venture and vast skies,
And in the chamber where he darkly slept,
Gradual and pale, the calm, sane light of dawn?.....

The WOMAN

Yours is the sign! You are the light!

HERAKLES

At last!.....
How I have sought you! O is it you indeed?
And do you bring me news at last and welcome—
News of myself and welcome to the Lord?
O can I rest assured that even now
The Lord wakes in his chamber silently,
And like a stranger and athirst for love,
And all aflame to know and to be known?.....
Know you indeed the Lord? and is he there,
The one true perfect friend, who is most friendless;—
The matchless lover, whose love none receives,
And who is loved of none? Look in my eyes!
Tell me the light is there — that I am He!.....

The WOMAN

... .You are the strength, the light, the life, — the Lord!
What shall I do that I may love you?

The POET

Speak!
Have you the strength? Have you the light—the life?

HERAKLES

speaking to the WOMAN alone

Only believe and all shall yet be well!
Love and believe! I have no more than faith
To guide me, and no more to comfort me
Than love,—and mine is still the greater need!
Mine is the greater need, for mine, at last,
Mine is the greater strength! The strength is there—
The secret strength I almost fear to feel!
Measureless is the strength and merciless—
And like a child whose eyes are vague with sleep,
Haunted with dreams and dazed with real light;—
Whose mind, with dark pre-natal memories,
Is still perplexed, and hardly yet evolved
From ancient error and the brutal grasp
Of fear, force, falsehood, destiny, and death;—
Who is not yet self-realized, self-assured,
Conscious and calm in thought, in aim, in will.
Yet, as I must believe, do you believe,
And all shall come to pass, and all be well!.....

The WOMAN

I love and I believe! I see the light;
I feel the strength that will not stay or spare;
I know the Lord; I know that he shall come
To bring me the good news!

HERAKLES

O be assured

Of victory! I love you! I shall come
Again to you.....Be faithful till I come!

A MAN

What do they say?

A HARLOT

He bids her "Be thou faithful
Until I come!"

All laugh except HERAKLES, the WOMAN, and the POET, who remain thrilled, startled, and absorbed.

The POET

I scarce believe—and yet
He spoke as one having authority,
Having the truth's commandment clear as light
And blind as light and undissuadable;—
Being in strength creative as a God!
How shall I know?.....

The WOMAN

conscious only of HERAKLES

You will not leave me—now?

HERAKLES

I leave with you one who is more than I—
Even the soul—even the Spirit of Truth!.....
He shall be with you always to the end,
Who is the guide, the way, the comforter!

HERAKLES

I may not rest: I love you and must go.
He shall bear witness in my stead. At last
I shall return:—and let there be a light,
His light undimmed to guide me to his house!
Be faithful—lest he fall again on sleep!

The WOMAN

I cannot leave you! Lord, I will not stay
Where you are not!—You are the way, the life;
You are the truth!

HERAKLES

I shall perchance be true
At last and perfect!.....Now, there is within me
Labour and violence, ruin and redemption.
My soul is an invaded citadel,
A precinct where contending armies wait,
Fierce and resolved,—the death-grip is still toward!.....
And if I win at all it shall be hard!
This very hour all is in jeopardy:—
The dark whirls in my vision even now;
And like the rumour of resurgent tides
I hear the ancient curse of error cry
Up well-worn estuaries of the shaken mind!.....

Suddenly voices are heard crying in the distance, and a confused rumour as of some great commotion in the city.

FIFTH SCENE

IOLAUS

Lord!— do you hear? Some mischief is afoot!
The city cries as with a single voice!—
What can it be? Some great event has chanced.....
I'll find the cause of this and come again.

IOLAUS hastens away.

HERAKLES

.....What great event concerns me save the soul?
And none cry in the Agora because
The soul of man at last comes to its own!

Again from the city rises a vast rumour of voices.

Hark!.....In my heart I hear their cries resound!
They are my soldiers and my people! Hark!.....
There in this hour my plumed battalions wait
Their leader, and my citizens their King.
They know not and they will not understand
Whither away I am gone on so far
Without them,—I, who shall not now return!.....
The die is cast, and, come what may, I take
The bounty of ambitious destinies
To be my birthright, nor shall Gods or men
Force and delude me from my utmost goal!

Again is heard the voice of a distant multitude.

The POET

How they cry out upon us, — all the world!

HERAKLES

.....Crying in vain! — O let me stay no more!
For still my heart, to hear the voice of the world —
My world of youth and conquest and renown —
Crying upon me, suffers and is not strong,
As the great heart of perfect love must be!
O, lest the good great moment, lest the vision,
Lest the redemption, now at last begun,
Suffer some wrong by reason of the heart's
Weakness and all my life's remembered joys,
Let me go forth away from them, away
From all that was and is, to what shall be —
Which, in this primal morning of the soul,
Thro' widening gateways of deliverance,
With endless promise cheers the forward way!.....

The WOMAN

Suffer me, and constrain me not to be
Without you! There is place for me to follow
Where you may go.....

HERAKLES

There are no followers
Nor captains on the soul's eternal quest!

The POET

Yet, if the torch go forward in your hand,
Shall not its splendour serve to guide us on?

FIFTH SCENE

Well may we question, who have sought so long,
Where you will go and whither is the way.

HERAKLES

Mine is my way and yours must be your own.
Ask me no more, nor wonder if my words
Are strict and stern —

The POET

I know the truth is hard,
Neither compassionate of any grief
Or hope or weakness or imperfect joys.
But to that soul which bears the truth, in chief,
Truth is relentless! And I say to you
That if you have not now already paid
Abundantly the incalculable cost,
Then you shall pay even to the uttermost!

HERAKLES

What is the price of truth?

The POET

What is the truth?—
There is the question!

HERAKLES

He shall answer it,
And only he who earns the right to say,

HERAKLES

"I am the Truth!" — for he alone is true.
I stand in the beginning, and the way
Is hardly to be seen before my feet,
Which they must tread wherever it may go!.....
Ask me no questions, therefore, of the end.

The WOMAN

I am not curious, and I have no thought
Of mercy, and I have no other way
Than your way, Lord!.....

HERAKLES

O sacred human heart!
Come with me if you will, as best you may.
You are my witness how the sepulchre
Was rent and in his shroud the Sleeper stirred;
And how the prison door stood wide ajar
While momently, at least, lay out in light
The prospect of the soul's prosperities! —
You are my witness, and my heart wills well
That you, O Heart of faith! should share with me
Truth's gospel and the soul's new testament; —
Till, at the last, the Sleeper's dreams are done,
And he is waked and risen and on his way!.....

IOLAUS appears, coming in great haste.

IOLAUS

Lord! Lord!.....I bring you news —

FIFTH SCENE

HERAKLES

Who brings me news
Is welcome, if his news be news indeed!—
You all who have been with me in this hour,
You know how rashly I am hazarded,
As yet with no least knowledge of the way,
Into the free, far spaces of the soul!
I go because the wind is in my sails—
But chartless, helmless, on a shadowed sea;—
And haply I shall find the fabulous
Fair Paradise of truth, and hand in hand
With the grave Gods walk perfectly at last!.....
And haply I may shipwreck on the shores
Of circumstance and dark necessities!.....
Only the strength within me is assured,—
The strength of Herakles! All else is doubt.....
And O my spirit is fain of news!

IOLAUS

The King
Demands your presence in the Agora.

A MAN

to his companions

The King?.....He said the King!

A HARLOT

in an awed voice

What man is this?

HERAKLES

The King? — No public cares concern me now.
What will the King with me?

IOLAUS

I know but this:
An embassy comes hither from Eurystheus,
Sovereign of Argos. Heedless of the King,
They will not speak at his command; instead
They say their message is alone for you.

HERAKLES

Go on before me, I will shortly come;
Leave me, for I have need to be alone.

The WOMAN

Lord.....

HERAKLES

For a little, leave me. I will come.
This much is certain, that I will be free!
And therefore I will come to bid farewell
To rank and power and every servitude.
I will not heed the cost of what may bring
Deliverance. Leave me! I will shortly come —
And find you there where the world waits for me!.....

After a moment of hesitation they all depart: the POET first, then the WOMAN and IOLAUS; lastly the little crowd from the tavern. As these last are leaving they pause a moment to look at HERAKLES.

FIFTH SCENE

A MAN

My Lord, forgive me if I question you —
What is your name?

HERAKLES

Men call me Herakles.

The men and women depart, leaving HERAKLES alone.

End of the Fifth Scene.

SIXTH SCENE

This scene immediately follows the preceding in time. The sun is only just risen.

Thebes. Before the house of HERAKLES.

MEGARA stands upon the threshold of the open door.

SIXTH SCENE

MEGARA

The golden wings of light beat up the sky;
The stars are set; the dew-fall and the dawn
Are everywhere, quiet as benediction;
The earth's fresh perfumes, like an incense, rise
Into the windless, universal air;
And even the old, blank city ways are still
And flushed like pathways in love's paradise.....
It is morning! — and my lover is not come!

A pause. MEGARA sings.

She waited in the bride-chamber;
    Her face was young and clear as light;
    Her lips were sensuous and bright; —
The Bridegroom came not unto her.

She kept fresh flowers in the room;
    Her eyes were spacious as the sea;
    And thro' the open casement she
Kept vigil till her Lord should come.

She saw the stars go up the sky;
    The sunlight and the moonlight were

Like crowns and chaplets in her hair;—
She would not break her faith to die.

She set a signal in the day;
She set a beacon in the night;
The guarded flame of love burned white
And single in her heart alway.

She waited in the bride-chamber:
Her hair was soft as sleep; her breast
Was tranquil, like a place of rest.....
The Bridegroom came not unto her.

"His heart," she said, "is here at home;
"His love, I know, abides with me;
"And he would choose his bride to be
"Prepared and perfect should he come."

She waited in the lonely years;
The bride-chamber was all her room;
She dreamed not of another doom;
She had no thought or time for tears.

And when the Bridegroom came at last
And found his Bride serene and strong,
He said, "Beloved, I tarried long,
"But now despair and doubt are passed."

She said, "I know not what you mean;
"I have no part with suffering
"Or grief or fear; a better thing
"Life cannot be than mine has been!

"For I have lived with Truth and Love,
"And all my life was beautiful
"And strong and fortunate and full
"And great and good and glad thereof!"

A pause.

Friendless he seemed — inimical and strange
And splendid, when his angered strength cast down
The diadem and scorned the pride of kings!
Yet wherefore were his rapture and his rage?
Why was he so tremendous and estranged
And resolute last night against us all?
Where is he now — and when shall he return.....
My heart is like a place of desolation,
And like a lost child in a woful place;
The jealous depths of love are calm no more,
After last night, but shaken and dismayed.....
I would to God he were come home to me!

She pauses to gaze about her and then returns slowly into the house. A moment after, HERAKLES appears.

HERAKLES

O bland and tranquil human habitation,

HERAKLES

Fortunate house of happiness and love,
Where love is life and life is love, where truth
Is very tender and exquisite as song,
And where the meaning of the Mystery
Is simply and ineffably revealed!—
O treasure-house of kind and serious joys,
Hushed, holy house of peace, my house, my home!—
I know not in my heart what nameless fear
Afflicts me as mine eyes behold you now!
Is it perhaps the dread that hence from you
Lies the new promise of the forward way,
And hence the issue, and the sunrise hence?
Yet, in the clear accounting of all things,
I have no guess what voyage of the soul
Could take me hence from you, O tranquil house!—
O mother of my children, O my sons,—
My little sons, so fair and young,—from you!
Is not the best of being here at home?—
The candour and the loveliness of life;
Beauty and innocence of days; and all
The wise, warm, ancient virtues of the heart,
And all the peace of the prodigious soul?.....
O Well-beloved, the whole heart's yield of flowers
Perfumes the quiet chambers where you sleep!.....
My love is with you, and my dearest thought
Is of you, and where you are there am I
In spirit and in love!.....I will not fear!
This is the loveliest and most bountiful

Of all good fortune of man's mortal life:
Surely it shall not for the truth's sake pass
Out of the sum of real prosperities!
Rather my loved ones and my love shall share,
Always with me and to whatever end,
The days and ways of the enfranchised soul!

A moment's pause. Then he calls:

Megara!

MEGARA appears in the doorway.

MEGARA

Herakles!—at last! at last!

She runs forward to greet him.

My love — my dear, dear love — at last come home!

HERAKLES

Is not my whole heart always here at home?

MEGARA

O welcome, welcome! — As it was with me
When I first loved you, so it is to-day!
You come to me as after many days,
After long, anxious, heart-sick days of doubt.....
My heart was like a house of mourning: now
There is rejoicing and the sound of song,
The light of festival! — The Well-beloved
Returns at last, the Bridegroom is at hand!

HERAKLES

O come into my arms! I seem to feel
Beat in your breast the strong and simple heart,
The faithful and inveterate heart of life,
Which animates with the bright blood of being
The diverse fruit of earth's vast pregnancies!.....

They embrace. A slight pause.

Where are my sons?

MEGARA

They hardly wake from sleep.
One called you in the night, speaking your name.

HERAKLES

My children!.....And my Love! O Megara,
Say that you love me always to the end!

MEGARA

I love you to whatever end may come,
Ever and always and without reprieve!

HERAKLES

Then, and in silence, hear me to the last.
I know how little truth is speakable;
And I shall hardly find, for all my pains,
Language sufficient to express the soul;—
Yet it may be your love shall understand!—
Last night you saw me and you heard me speak.

SIXTH SCENE

Wonder no more because I cast away
The crown! — for even last night I was assured
That in the compass of the soul's ambition,
In the resources of man's utmost strength,
In the dim, secret treasure-house of thought,
There were perfections more supreme, desires
More absolute, achievements more divine,
Than any that the world is witness of!.....
Then did I blindly wreak my inmost will,
And had no understanding of my deeds.
But in the dawn, — O, in the morning, — then
I found the very truth, as in a vision! —
The light! — and I was plainly justified,
And perfectly; for this is truth's first lesson,
And easiest, and least of price, — that all
Business and pleasure and preferment, fame
And government and grandeurs of this world
Are but the toys with which the mind of man
Beguiles the leisures of its infancy.
Who knows the mind's austere maturities,
The heart's full-grown intensities; — who sees
The treasures of the Spirit, fabulous
Beyond imagination; — I believe
Naught else, to him, is profitable at all —
No triumphs, glories, kingdoms, amplitudes
Of fortune, pleasures, majesties, dominions!
I am but newly waked into the light;
My way begins, — my way, my hope, my hazard.

HERAKLES

For truly I have found myself at last,
And in myself a promise more supreme
And an inheritance more bountiful
Than thought can understand or faith believe!.....
Self-mastered to some purpose more than mine,
In the first morning, with the soul's first-fruits
I come to you!—O brave wise heart of love,
Surely you shall not fear to share with me
The best, hereafter, and the best alone:
Love, labour, and the fierce incertitudes!.....

MEGARA

Hardly I guess the meaning of your words.
And well it may be that in spite of all
I shall not understand even at last.....
Yet take me — keep me — lead me to your light!
My sons and you and I, — we are one life,
One love, one being,—naught shall make us twain!

HERAKLES

I also know not what my words may mean.....
I know not what the price of truth may be,
Or what the cost of man's perfection is
To man, or how the soul is satisfied.
I know but this: that ever and evermore
I shall not rest!.....O it may come to pass
That if you love me you shall die of it —
As who shall not before the Journey's end?

For thus we die to live perpetually!.....
And even it well may be, for all I know,
That only in exceeding bitter sorrow
Are we so slain and sacrificed and saved!—
That all with heavy labour and cruel cost
The soul must reap in life's neglected fields
The living bread, and in untended vineyards
Press from ripe fruit the consecrated wine,
Which are its livelihood. Who knows how hard
The truth's divine imperatives shall prove?
Courage, strong heart! Be sure there is no more
That must be done than man at best can do!
And if you find yourself, as well you may,
Best in the strong sublimity of love,—
O then come with me to the perfect end!.....

MEGARA

What have I else in all my life to do?—
Your spirit is my strength, your heart my refuge!

HERAKLES

Megara!.....O it may be we shall win,
And come into the heritage! At least
We shall go on in the fair-way till death,
Serious and stedfast and supremely one!

The SONS OF HERAKLES appear in the doorway of the house.

MEGARA

.....In the fair-way till death!

HERAKLES

My Love!

He perceives his children, who issue from the doorway.

My sons!

HERAKLES tenderly embraces the children.

A MESSENGER appears.

The MESSENGER

Herakles! — Lord! — The envoys of Eurystheus,
Sovereign of Argos, stand before the King—

HERAKLES

Why are you come to me?

The MESSENGER

They will not speak
Their master's message save alone to you.
Therefore the summons of the King is sent
To bid you straightway to the Agora.

HERAKLES

The Agora!.....Liberty is beyond!.....
Thro' and beyond my path of freedom leads.

SIXTH SCENE

He turns to MEGARA and the children.

Come, Well-beloved — let us go down together.
For they must take farewell of the rank world
Who walk their own ways into Paradise!......

End of the Sixth Scene.

SEVENTH SCENE

Early morning. The beginning of this scene and the preceding scene are contemporaneous.

Thebes. The Agora.

In the Agora are CREON *and* ALCMENA, *seated and surrounded by a body of soldiers. Immediately before the King stands* AMPHITRYON; *at some distance beyond stand the* MESSENGERS OF EURYSTHEUS, *three in number. The rest of the Agora is filled by a vast concourse of people.*

SEVENTH SCENE

AMPHITRYON

They come safe-guarded as Ambassadors,
As envoys of Eurystheus — to my son.

ALCMENA

To Herakles.....

AMPHITRYON

With insolence and pride
They dare recall our kinship and proclaim
Herakles subject of the Argive King;
Yet sworn to silence save to him they seek,
By no persuasions will their lips disclose
The serious purpose of their embassage.

AMPHITRYON seats himself beside the King.

CREON

These are strange tidings; and the veil that masques
The face of destiny seems dark indeed.....

AMPHITRYON

I fear their silence and their proud reserve.
What can their message be to Herakles?

CREON

What to their message shall your son reply?
Not in the vulgar press of circumstance
Is fate concealed, but in the soul of man!
And we have seen, last night, into the soul
Of Herakles enough, at least, to make
The question poignant and the doubt supreme!

ALCMENA

Last night!.....I thought a stranger stood before me
Clothed in the likeness of my son.....To-day
I dare not guess what dark catastrophe
The Gods prepare to try his secret strength,
To thwart his undivined, misguided will!

CREON

I fear no secret message, nor the stroke
Of adverse fortune, nor the coward heart
Or evil purpose of Eurystheus' hate,
Nor dark catastrophe;—I fear the man
Who struck the crown of kingship from his brows
And gave us earnest of the soul's ambition!
Man fashions fate after his own design;
And in his likeness, as a mirror is,
The face of life is featured and expressed;
And he deciphers on a vacant page
His sense, his story, his significance.
Who can predict what Herakles shall see

When he lays bare the future's shrouded face?
Who can foretell what sense his soul shall find,
What stately meaning, what majestic myth,
Inscribed on life's familiar palimpsest?

ALCMENA

He is beyond recognizance!.....My love's
Maternal arms feel vacant of my son!

CREON

.....I have played the game out to its mean mild end,
And won the world's prize, in a certain measure.
Now, being quit with fortune and grown old,
I am no longer partisan,—as needs
Man must be when his stake is in the game,—
But, disabused of life's persuasions, which
O'erbalance justice in its own defence,
I sit apart in the clear empty light
Of wisdom, as in some pale aftermath,
And grow, in justice and serenity,
Clearly and patiently contemplative.
Therefore I find for this emergency
Some thoughts which come not all inaptly in
To help our understanding of the man
Who yesternight was strange unto us all.
For I have lately, in the liberal years,
Foregone the lore of cheap philosophies
Which find an ultimate identity

In all the souls and destinies of men.
Crowds are but numbers; and at last I see
There are not merely players of the game;
There is not, high or low, only the one
Sensible and substantial prize to which
The fiat of the world gives currency,—
And which, in various ways, is always won!
There is besides the one, estranged, rare man,
Whose light of life is splendid in the soul,
Burns with a kind of glory in his strength,
And gives such special grandeur to ambition,
That he will make no terms with fortune, nor
Play for whatever prize the game affords.
He thinks to vanquish destiny, enforce
The Gods, and, by transcendent strength and toil,
Earn — what alone of all things must be earned —
The soul's prize — which is always just the soul! —
The soul, self-mastered, self-assured, self-known,
God-like! and with the deathless Gods co-heir
Of truth's ineffable eternities; —
The soul, despised, neglected and concealed,—
And yet, in truth, as in his raptured mind,
Perhaps the great prize — which is always lost!
And therefore, wisdom says, no prize at all!
But merely, for the common use of life,
A fatal lure, a frenzied hope, a dream
And madness of imaginative minds.....
So is the world's work justified! And last,

SEVENTH SCENE

Now, when the game of life is played — and lost, —
Lost in the main, yet somehow hurried through
To the calm, threadbare, tolerable end, —
The humour of the thing comes quietly home,
As we discern how wise we were to take
The loss for granted — and enjoy the game!
We learn our weakness; learn to thank the Gods
That we were weak and had no prospect of
The prize, no lonely and supreme ambitions;
Learn, at the last, on what fantastic terms
Life is a conflict, since in fate's despite
All men may yet prove victor — save the strong!
The irony, to man's maturer mind,
Sorts with his ancient pleasant sense of things.
He marks the stress of gross necessities,
Immedicable and unalterable,
Which shape the trifling destinies of man;
He finds an average of circumstance,
Equal to all men in the true last test;
He learns how much, by temperance and fear,
The weak men of the world persuade the Gods;
And smiling with a mild and undeceived
Despair, he sees the strong men of the soul
Enforce the times to their discomfiture,
And, of the primal stuff of circumstance,
With which the long life of a common man
Is very comfortably compromised,
Contrive their stately and remorseless ruin!

HERAKLES

Yes!.....he discerns, beyond his private fault
And failure, — when the game is played, and lost, —
Where thought turns sick and dizzy and dismayed
On the black borders of its own abyss, —
How all men living are not ever free,
But straitly prisoned in the Mystery,
Burdened beneath the universal strength,
Merged in the flux of dark infinities.....
Which are the Gods! — in whose relentless grasp
The strong man strives and strangles and is slain.
Then, to his humour, men resemble most
Dull creatures who live down at the dense, dark,
Fathomless, dumb foundations of the sea, —
Who, if they are not pliant, and too weak,
Too yielding to resist, are broken and burst,
Crushed out of life under the passionless,
Insuperable weight of the element
In which they live and move and have their being.
Are we not justly, then, and terribly
Enough — however much we see the joke! —
Cautioned to bear with wise humility
The utmost rigours of unyielding chance,
And meet the serious issues of the soul
As I have done — with a mild gayety,
An unambitious mind and a lax will!
So may we prosper to some worldly end;
So may we gain assured maturities
And aptitudes for a well-ordered life;

So, in the lesson of many years, at last,
We earn some sense of what the Gods can do,
At best or worst, to ruin or redeem.
And therefore, by the witness of his words
Last night, I find our Herakles imperilled
Not by the Gods but by himself alone! —
For the strong man no calculus computes,
No reason reckons, no arithmetic
Demonstrates or foresees by any means. .
Only we know there is no mortal peril
So dire, so desperate as to be strong!

AMPHITRYON

You are the King! and may, by word and deed,
Give aid and counsel to my son.

CREON

Alas!.....
Who is a King to counsel or advise,
To help or hinder, if a man's free will
Furthers and guides and justifies his being?
The strong receive no help as they are strong;
They spare not — and they are not ever spared
By Gods or men; the counsel of the wise,
The tender tears of love's solicitude,
Cannot deter them or persuade them home!
Alas! Strength is a hazard none may share,
A genius none may caution or advise.

HERAKLES

The strong man and the humble man are twain
By the one real division of men's lives
And destinies: there a great gulf is fixed,
A dark abyss no rainbow-bridge can span,
Between life's level places of brief hopes,
Familiar ways, and measurable ends,
And the starred skies of thought's imagination.
To you my kingship seems a proper prize
For life's fulfilment; — but last night we learned
How the ambitious soul scorns to deserve
Life's facile, fortunate prosperities.
I think to such a one the purpose of
His will, the strength that marks his isolation,
Are to him as a passion — as a vision
Of truth, which gives his strange soul liberty
To flame its furtherance thro' the wise world!.....
Vainly for his advantage we discern
How, soon or late, with ancient irony,
The wise world, sitting at the spectacle,
Hails his surrender or his helpless ruin.
For when the mad light dawns, the waking soul
Endures no lesson save its own, receives
No truth save what itself exemplifies!

Suddenly the POET and the WOMAN appear in the open space before CREON. They are so self-absorbed that they seem unconscious of the world about them.

SEVENTH SCENE

The POET

My heart is nervous like a place of peril.....

The WOMAN

My heart is quiet like a place of peace.
I see the light; I know he is the Lord.

The POET

Faintly I feel the promise of the Dawn
Pale on the prison windows of the soul;
And I believe, secluded in his strength,
Dazed in his light, it well may be the Lord
Is waking in the house of Herakles!.....
Whose faith shall perfectly shine out to help
My unbelief?.....Whose witness is at hand
To certify the Truth and prove the Lord?.....

He looks about him and realizes where he is.

This is the Agora.....The King — the world —
The envoys of Eurystheus — all are here!
And we are here, who keep his vigil! — and
Hither, at last, the man shall grandly come!.....

CREON

Stranger, be welcome! By your chance strange words
I dare surmise you come from Herakles?

The POET turns and faces CREON.

The POET

After a moment's silence

O King!—you, who are old; whose eyes have seen,
Borne on the shoulders of subjected men,
The little pageant of the world go by,
Pontifical and proud, with Gods and gold
And bright caparisons of victory—
And nothing come of it! — whose ears have heard,
Beyond the high, hard music of the march,
Beyond the chorus and the canticles,
The strange, strained sob of the great human heart,
Crushed and subdued against the iron breast
Of life's obscure, supreme necessities,—
The wailing and the bitter, broken cry
Of souls disconsolate and lives foredoomed
To ruin and intolerable wrong
From Gods and men — and nothing come of it! —
You, who may haply, in your whole long life,
Once and at last have dreadfully discerned
The infinite, inscrutable darkness
Bounding the narrow precincts of the mind,
And the old, awful taciturnities,
Against whose smooth, impenetrable walls
The shouting and the singing voice of life
Shatter and die and are not heard beyond —
And nothing come of it! — O you, whose mind
Is wise with the long audience and vigil
Your life has been — and nothing come of it! —

What is your faith, and what shall be my hope
Of Herakles? Is it the very light
Of truth, the very strength of the soul's cause,
This woman has discerned radiant in him?
Is he the very guide our souls have sought
Out of the labyrinth? Is he the Saviour?—
Give me your faith, for I am sick with doubt.....
Are not the dire, dark Gods, the bitter Gods,
Ranged, leagued and armoured with the common
world
Of crowds and Kings to work the man's undoing?
Well I discern where the blind, brutal hand
Of fortune stretches at him from the shadow.....
And soon the stroke shall fall!.....Is it too soon?
Speak!—can he bear the blow? and is he yet
Full-grown in strength, and, like a God, become
Invulnerable?—or must he yield at last?
Or die far on the frontiers, overwhelmed?.....
Speak! Speak! My spirit is irresolute,
Swift and unstable as a wind-swept flame!
Give me your faith; the crucial hour is near;
He comes! He comes!—and wilful of his cause,
Here shall the soul take issue with the world!

CREON

After a slight pause; in his most temperate tones

Stranger, be welcome none the less because
You tax the patience of philosophy,

And vex a man whose age and whose estate
Give him some reason for the world's regard.
Patience may suffer; but my sole concern
Is with the perfect humour of the thing;
And since you variously enhance the joke,
Be gladly welcome! I discern in you
That taint of a poetic eloquence,
Which is perhaps the fashion of your youth,
And therefore to be leniently endured,
Yet gives a special tinge of irony
To the reflective mind which hears you speak.
Believe me, you might well be rid of it,
And of your flourish and intemperance
Of fancy, which the sane sense wearies of.
Whatever hazard of man's life is toward,
The facts are still sufficient to the end
In sight,—and ends invisible are just
Mere myth! That you impute to me a faith,
And, for yourself, indulge some fervent hope
In what vague ventures of the frenzied mind
No soothsayer of dreams can clearly tell,
Charms me—as youth will charm us!—but we find
A smile to vex down such extravagance!
Alas! we have some serious cause to fear
That the unhappy mind of Herakles
Is raptured and estranged — resolved to take
Some final issues with the Gods and men.

SEVENTH SCENE

But we have seen, what you at last may learn,
How such pretensions of the spirit fail, —
Whose victory, I take it, is your hope.
Life, like a candle in a starless night,
Brightens and burns, or flutters and is spent,
As man's wise weakness spares the guarded flame,
Or man's rash strength resolves in all despite
To lift his torch into the spacious winds,
To blaze his path across the darknesses,
And force the elements to his own undoing.....
Only the strong go forward — and are slain!
Only the strong, defenceless, dare — and die!
Only the strong, free, fain and fearless, — fail!
Remember this! lest a worse thing than mere
Passion and ecstasy of poems befall you.

The POET

Old man, old vain mild phantom of a man! —
These many years there is no phrase of all
Your cowardly smooth wit, no attitude
Of yours I have not learned and wearied of!
Poor ancient, philosophic humourist!
I know you as you pitiably are:
Wise as the world is wise, — and ignorant
As only the dull, blatant world can be!
Tell me your lies no more, your clever lies!
Is there a man so dull he has not felt
The countless soldiery of circumstance

Charge down out of the dark against us all?
Is there a man so blind he has not seen
How fearfully the timid citizens
Of the wise world that you are master of
Armour their nakedness against the foe?
Is there a man so false he has not learned
How all in vain men dress against the shafts
Of truth their shadow-shields, and all in vain
Shape for their lives' defence the seeming gold
Of faith, the shallow silver of a sane
Philosophy,—to fit the cultured mind!—
The dull, stern bronze of patient hardihood,
Or any base alloy or mean deceit
Of weakness and respectability,—
However tried and tempered in the forge
Of the remembered usage of the world,
Fed with felled branches from the tree of time?
Is there a man so false and blind and dull
He does not know how all confinements yield,
All fashions of defence are overborne,
When the real truth's Redeemer is at hand,—
When, midst the very ruins of the House
Of Fear, the mighty soul finds place and room?.....
In the great game where each man's stake is set,
They only lose who dare not ever play
For the one prize that is not counterfeit—
And they must always lose! Only the strong
Go forward—and are saved! Only the strong,

Restless, defenceless, and companionless,
Dare — and supremely live! Only the strong,
Free, fearless, all-ambitious, — by so much
Come to the soul's sublime inheritance!
I asked no stale philosophy like yours,
Safe and sententious; and I am not apt
To take your dreadful humour, — which to me
Seems like the simper on a dead man's face!
Out of my soul's unrest I cried to you!
Out of my weakness and my heart's desire
I cried for faith, to you who had it not! —
For faith that here at last, come to his own,
Is the true, brave, divine, enfranchised man!.....
I seek my saviour! I am nothing more
Than a great voice crying upon his name,
Shouting his welcome, — for he surely comes!
My poems are the pure pæan of his advent —
And well I know he sleeps within myself!
Still, tho' I call him with a constant voice,
And, standing heart-sick in the twilight, fill
His glimmering casement with free flights of song,
He wakes not yet for all that I can do!.....
Therefore, O therefore is my hope alive
For the true man in whom the saviour wakes,
Who is my equal, — who is more than I!.....
Till, at his touch, the golden gates of light
Sunder! — till, suddenly, the pregnant soul
Wakes in the pangs of God's nativity!.....

CREON

Poor mad, mazed, dream-bedevilled, frenzied fool! —
'T is well my anger is no longer rash —

The POET

Mad to your sense I may be, — mad almost
As God is mad to those who know Him not!.....

Turning to the WOMAN

Woman, O Woman! what shall be my hope?
Would that my faith were perfect! Overlong
My heart has fed with blood the sacred flame;
Mine eyes have kept the consecrated vigil; —
And almost seemed magnificently at last
To witness to the coming of the Lord!.....
O might the tranquil eyes of wisdom read
Into the powers and prospects of the soul
A larger sense of what is possible
Than I have seen — and help my unbelief!

The voices of a great multitude sound, crying out in the distance.

The VOICES

Herakles! Herakles!

The POET

At last he comes!

CREON

Comes to relieve our small suspense, to end
The prologue and enact the — comedy!

SEVENTH SCENE

The POET

moving swiftly to a position close beside the throne of CREON and addressing him with an earnest intensity

Old man, forego your childish pleasantries!
Your cap and bells ring sadly out of tune
Amid the solemn and celestial choirs
Which sound across their clear antiphonies,
Now as the Hero — and, it well may be,
The Saviour — yea! the truth's Redeemer comes!
Put by your mannered, threadbare attitude;
Put by your trifling wisdom of the world;
Witness and understand! Your eyes and brain
May well be clear, — for age wears out the world
In man's regard, like some embroidered silk
Worn threadbare in the gradual waste of time,
And leaves a calm, transparent vacancy,
As of pale light over a hueless sea.
Watch! and it may be you shall read the news
And see into the secret!.....

The VOICES

nearer than before

Herakles!
Herakles! Herakles!

The POET

He comes! — O King,
He is that man from whose resplendent eyes,

HERAKLES

But lately, to the woman who had faith,
The light of Gods shone out like a strange dawn!.....

The VOICES

always nearer

Herakles! Herakles!

The POET

Behold him well!
I — I have seen his strength, and half-believed
That he is of the few indomitable
Whom the Gods hardly bring into dominion
By any means! — till I have seemed to hear
Sound in my soul the trumpets of his triumph!.....

The VOICES

close at hand

Herakles! Herakles!

The POET

He is at hand!.....
The Bridegroom comes!..... O Heart! O Paranymph!
Let the sealed gates of love stand wide asunder,
And all the bounds of faith perish away!
And let the winged soul, from its lonely skies,
Cry out in joy, claiming the victory!

Amid a great roar of welcome from the people and the soldiers, HERAKLES appears in the open space before the King. He is accompanied by MEGARA and his Children, and followed by IOLAUS. He confronts the King and the cheering multitude in silence. Gradually the tumult subsides. Meanwhile the MESSENGERS OF EURYSTHEUS draw near the throne of CREON.

AMPHITRYON

Welcome, my son!

CREON

Thrice welcome, Herakles!
Messengers are come hither from the King
Of Argos, and will speak alone to you.

HERAKLES

It will not help that I should hear them now.
I have renounced all profits and concerns
And servitudes of proud and politic men;
For, in the strong fulfilment of my vision,
I am resolved hereafter to be free!
Therefore the envoys of Eurystheus
Now may depart in silence: I no more
Regard them, and I will not hear them now.
I must be diligent about my business,
Which brooks no more delay! — And know you well,
If you behold me now it is because
I have one thing in all the world, one thing
To all the world, and only one, to say:
Farewell!

HERAKLES

Rumour among the people and soldiers. The King and those about him listen with anxious concern.

My heart, this one, brief, utmost time,
Returns to where it once went proudly home
And daily dwelt, — knowing no better place,
No more majestic mansion of desire,
No costlier love, — to bid you all farewell!
Farewell! I linger but to take my leave
Of all I loved; my soul is on its way;
I am impatient to begone; — farewell!
Farewell! My road is hence and hard and far;
And where it leads me I may haply learn;
And whither, if at all, it takes me home!.....
Now I but know I will be free to follow
In the steep way, my soul's way, to the light —
The light which dawns within me! O my friends —
Kin, soldiers, citizens — be well assured
That even in this mystic and majestic hour
The Lord is in my house — and wakes!.....At dawn,
Solving the heart's incertitudes, one came
To witness to the Lord and specify
His advent — and he wakes — and all is well!
I asked — and bountifully I have received;
I sought — and I have wonderfully found;
I knocked — and now the spacious and sudden doors
Splendidly open to my furtherance!.....
I must begone! Farewell, at last, farewell!
My heart is fain; my will is on the way;

And, from the soul's eternal secret source,
Issues a strength I hardly dare to feel
Within me and upon me! — such a strength
As drives the ploughshare of its great resolve
Across the little limits of this world,
And may endure no let of God or man
Cast in the fair-way of its rash ambition!.....

CREON

Now sounds the dread, mad voice whose sense is peril.

The POET

Now sounds the trumpet-call of hope, the cry
Of the enfranchised, strong, expectant soul!

HERAKLES

Comrades and friends — companions of my youth —
Lovers of mine, whose love was health and home,
Honour and happiness to me, — farewell!
Now may your eyes discern the mystic change!
Him you behold is not that Herakles
You knew, who armed you from the temple walls,
And captained you across the battlefields,
In the dark way of death, to victory!
I am no more, no more, — O valiant sons
Of Cadmus! O my soldiers! — as I was
That day we wrapped in winding-sheets of flame
Palace and parapet and pinnacle
And all the bastioned power of proud Orchomenos!

I go away into the light from you;
I leave you; I return no more..... And yet
You shall remember how it was with us
That day the hero and the host returned
Full-flushed, in triumph, with the Minyan spoil! —
When the pale women caught our dreadful hands,
Where the red blood dried black, and wreathed our swords —
Our sinister, soiled swords of victory —
With bridal flowers, and kissed our fierce, parched mouths,
And, weeping, laughed into our shining eyes
With eager lips, song-spent and tremulous!
You shall remember! — and I leave with you
That Herakles who bids you now farewell!

An immense clamour rises from the people. The soldiers, with cries of devotion and dismay, rush forward and surround HERAKLES. They even seize his garments with restraining hands.

O manhood — memories — mood of many days
Of well-companioned tasks and victories
And exultations and familiar joys,
Evoked, impassioned in your hearts and mine! —
How shall I bear to say farewell to you?
Brothers-in-arms — O comrades — faithful friends —
It is not as my heart wills — not my heart
Is turned from you-ward! — for God knows my heart

Is yearning and irresolute and aggrieved,
And will not leave you, and laments and loves
And dares not lose what life has held so dear!
Only I know there is no way for me
But my way, and no way but yours for you;
And all ways of the world are false and blind
And barred and bounded to a mean ambition,
Which knows no more magnificent prize than mere
Exclusive profits and prosperities;
And all ways of the soul are ways of truth,
Which whoso treads them out shall learn to know
What excellence there is within himself
Which finds no hope or having tolerable
That all men may not share on equal terms!
But since, when once revealed, the truth forever
Is irremediable; and since I know
You will not come with me out of the world;
And since I may not go away with you,
Back from my prospect and my path; — farewell!
What tho' the strong heart breaks to feel your love?
Yet will the soul, the waking soul, be free!.....

Turning swiftly to MEGARA

O let us hasten hence!

Turning again to the soldiers and people, and speaking as though to all the world

Farewell! Farewell! —
Now and forevermore!

HERAKLES

Meanwhile the MESSENGERS OF EURYSTHEUS have approached. Now one of them advances alone toward HERAKLES.

The MESSENGER

O Herakles,
Wise is your purpose now to bid farewell
To all the world!

HERAKLES

Long since I took my leave
Of Kings and of the Messengers of Kings.

The MESSENGER

Wise is your purpose—for the proud fair days
And pleasant ways of life your feet have trod,
Are changed and ended to return no more.
Farewell — O bid farewell indeed to all
These high commandments, riches, fame and friends,
Honour and eager glories of the world!
Farewell — O bid farewell to happiness;
To home and wife and child a last farewell!

HERAKLES

Rashly you speak of what you know not of.
No man alive is justified to say
What things are fit for the self-centred soul.
I bid farewell to all that is not truth
And all enslavements of the soul,— but love

SEVENTH SCENE

Of two hearts blent together to one end
Of ecstasy and truth's eternities,
Is a great thoroughfare of liberty
Wherein the soul may walk its way well-pleased!
I bid farewell to none who go their ways,
Strong and resolved, wherever the light is.
To you, but not to them whose way is love,
Whose love is truth, I bid a last farewell.

The MESSENGER

Vain are your words, and all your thoughts are
vain,
And all your hopes! O bid farewell to love,
Farewell to friendship and to hope farewell,—
Farewell, a long farewell to liberty!
No more of all these things your life shall be
Made glad and great and good! — no more! no more!
But rather inconsolable solitude,
Hardship and hunger, shame and ill-report,
Vile words and bitter usage of the world,
Labour and servitude and sacrifice,
Vigil and vagrancy shall be your lot,
Your strength's achievement and your life's reward!

The POET

to the WOMAN, grasping her arm

Watch! for the death-grip comes, — more terrible
Than fear can image or despair conceive!.....

HERAKLES

Watch! for the dark, fierce, dread, revengeful Gods,
Out of the shadow of the Mystery,
Launch the lean lightnings of their utmost wrath!

HERAKLES

Farewell to love?..... Farewell to liberty?.....
And what of truth?..... And what of life itself?.....
Enough! Enough! These idle, senseless words
Merely perplex my purpose. Go your ways!
I have too long delayed to hear you, — go!

The MESSENGER

advancing a step toward HERAKLES

Born homeless by your sire's misdeeds, outcast
And exiled kinsman of the Argive King, —
Herakles! Herakles! — by birth, by race,
By right his subject, — pause and hear me speak!
For I am charged to bear the King's commands
To you, his servant —

HERAKLES

Silence! By the Gods —

The MESSENGER

The Gods enforce you to your Sovereign's will!

CREON

to the POET

See how he glares!

SEVENTH SCENE

The POET

His eyes are like a cry
Of horror! — like a stricken, haunted place!.....

HERAKLES

to himself

.....Where is the light?.....the light?.....

To the MESSENGERS, with violence

Begone! Begone!
I know my lineage; but I have no care
Of crowds or crowns or human servitudes!
Your King's commands are senseless words to me;
Your vain pretensions like an idiot's dream!
Enough! Begone! I have my soul to seek,
My truth to learn, my liberty to win,—
And all my labours are as yet undone!

The MESSENGER

Where are your labours?

HERAKLES

Where the light is not
To bring the light; and where the way is shut
To open out the way; and where the house
Is tenantless to rouse the Lord within! —
There are my labours and my works are these!

HERAKLES

The MESSENGER

By strict enforcement of Eurystheus' will
And stern commandment of the deathless Gods,
Yours are the labours of a subject man,
Yours are the tasks and toil of servitude!
For where Eurystheus bids your strength to serve,
There shall your works be done; and all shall reap
Plentiful harvests of your sowing, all
Shall profit where your single strength has earned!
And, from the world's avid and thrifty hand,
No wage shall you receive, even at last, —
And no thanksgiving......

HERAKLES

Silence! —

The MESSENGER

Herakles!
Herakles! by my voice your Sovereign speaks!
Teach your rebellious knees to kiss the dust;
Learn to obey, and humbly serve his will!

HERAKLES

Silence! Begone! —

To himself

What voice of prophecy
Cries in my heart?.....I dare not know the truth,
Nor hear the secret answered in my soul!
It were too monstrous if the worst were true —

SEVENTH SCENE

Too monstrous! I will doubt no more — and yet
Where is the light — my light?..... Where is the voice,
The one puissant voice of the soul's song?.....
Why am I left in darkness and alone,
Deserted and betrayed?..... Why do I feel
Shudder within me like a dreadful ghost
The superstition of a fatal thing?.....

The POET

I know the truth, I read the secret now!.....

CREON

starting to his feet

God! he will yield!.....

AMPHITRYON

My son!

MEGARA

My Herakles!

HERAKLES

turning upon her

You? — You? —

The POET

O were he strong enough to yield!

The WOMAN

throwing herself at the feet of HERAKLES

Lord, I believe!

HERAKLES

Your faith destroys me!

The WOMAN

Lord! —
Lord! — I believe!

HERAKLES

Then help my unbelief!
I dare not realize what the truth may be! —
So terrible it is, I half believe
There is some passing madness in my mind
By which the light is quenched, the voice is quelled!
Surely it must be so! I know but this,
I cannot see the light — and suddenly
All the serene and mighty symphonies
Of heart and brain and being are silent.....

The WOMAN

Lord!.....
Lord!.....I believe!

HERAKLES

.....The light returns — the voice!.....
I dare not understand!.....I dare not yield!.....

The MESSENGER
striking HERAKLES with his staff

Down in the dust, and do your master's will!

SEVENTH SCENE

The people and soldiers cry out with a mighty voice. With the swiftness of passion, HERAKLES wrests the staff from the hand of the MESSENGER and strikes him to the ground, where he lies insensible.

HERAKLES

utterly giving way to anger

Intolerable! Intolerable! — Beware,
O Gods, O Kings, O men who try me thus!
You play like children with a deadly thing!
That heart may learn to hate you which should love;
That strength may ruin which might best redeem!

Turning upon the two MESSENGERS who still confront him

Back to your kennel and your currish king!
I spare your lives which are not worth my pains!
Say to Eurystheus I may well return
From exile! — and should Herakles return,
Not one in Argos would survive to tell
The monstrous story of its devastation!.....
I would tear Tiryns from its base and cast
Its burned-out ruins on the Argive plain;
And in its place I would rear up a tower
Of the charred corpses of its citizens,
Welded in blood; and on its pinnacle
The pale head of Eurystheus should display
How he went down to death beneath my hand,

HERAKLES

Frenzied with fear, forsaken, false, accursed! —
Go! while there still is mercy in me, go!

A great shout of relief and acclamation rises from the soldiers and people. The POET springs forward and confronts HERAKLES face to face.

The POET

shouting at HERAKLES

Coward and traitor! Traitor! —

He is roughly seized by the soldiers; struggling in their grasp, he turns to the WOMAN

Mourn! O mourn,
Daughter of desolation, mourn your loss!
O faithful heart! — Woman! — We are betrayed!
Alas! Alas! He is as one of us,
Who all are slaves and dare not undergo
The mighty labours of our liberation!
He too is abject, feeble, and afraid;
He too with mean economy prefers
The helot's hovel to the master's house;
He too will not afford the price of truth
Nor earn the soul's full freedom by his pains!

HERAKLES

fiercely, but dismayed

Whose voice assails me?

SEVENTH SCENE

The POET

Mine!—which might have sung
Pæans and poems of you in exultation!

HERAKLES

Now by the Gods you well may die for this!.....

The POET

Slay if you will! Yet mind you well that he
Who slays himself in spirit and in truth,
Has done more murder than a sword can do!
I fear you not! — but fear me well you may,
Since I am one whose lips have learned to phrase
The truth's tremendous syllables of song!
Coward and traitor!—you have quenched the light
Of truth and shut the door of liberty!

HERAKLES stands, sobered and dizzy as from a blow. The soldiers begin to drag the POET away; he turns once more to the WOMAN.

Daughter of desolation, mourn your loss!
Weep, for the Child is slain! He slays the Child,
The Child of Light, about whose mystic birth
You were the mid-wife and the ministrant!.....

The WOMAN
to HERAKLES, with agony

Lord, I believe!

HERAKLES

What faith can make me whole?.....

The POET

as he is dragged away by the soldiers

Coward and traitor! — Traitor! —

His voice is suddenly silenced; he disappears. HERAKLES stands, heedless of everything; silent, sick, uncertain.

End of the Seventh Scene.

EIGHTH SCENE

Later of the same day. An open space before a Temple situated on an acropolis in Thebes. The gay tumult of a public holiday rises from the city, which lies out in panorama not far below.

The POET and the WOMAN, alone.

EIGHTH SCENE

The POET

We two in all the world have tears for him!.....
Hark! how they make a public festival
And cry thanksgiving that the God is slain.....

He pauses. The WOMAN is silent. The rumour from the city sounds louder than before.

Yes, they rejoice! — an excellence is lost,
And so their triumph is securely won!
Hark! how they mock with mirth the soul's defeat,
These dreadful, dread majorities of men
Who shout into the air and beat their hands
At pageants, tragedies, and crucifixions; —
Who, when a soul surrenders, sound across
Truth's broken harmonies their rank applause!

The cries of the multitude sound nearer.

Hark! Hark! They come — wreathed, radiant, unashamed!
Their drums sound hither where the mourners sit,
Sanctified, silent in their mystic grief,
About the gravestone of the earth-born God!
And whensoever, from the huddled homes,
The congregations and the courts of men,

One, rising up from where he sat so long
In darkness with the wise men of the world,
Finds God incarnate in his inmost soul,
And feels across the vision of his eyes
The unimagined, strong, seraphic light,
And speaks his mystic message thrilled with song,—
Then will you hear sound out against the man
The world's ironic, base, and vacant voice,—
The tuneless tumult of democracies!
So, when the soul is crushed, defeated, slain,—
O then as now, toward the crystalline
Unmindful heaven's serene immensity,
From all the nameless numbers of the world
Thunder their triumph and their acclamations!.....

A great, gay multitude of men and women, with CREON and AMPHITRYON at their head, appear on their way from the city to the Temple.

Not even here is sanctuary..... Behold!
They come to thank the Gods that God is slain!

CREON, on his way, perceives the POET and pauses.

CREON

Here's our poetic, pale enthusiast,
Changed from his madness, sobered, let us hope,
And somewhat wiser. Ah, how vain were all
Our hopes and fears! He merely boasted! What?—
Believed his boast, you say?—I grant you! Well,

And what of that? True faith's the only harm!
For much as Herakles was crazed by dreams,
So in their lives are many men deceived, —
And by their disenchantment much matured!
Thus we discern when excellence is lost
How much is saved, — our hero first of all!
And last; but not; good sir, believe me, least,
We now may pleasantly observe how well
Our sense of humour and our quiet smile
Of irony still vindicate their use,
And prove life's ablest critics after all!

The POET listens with quiet indifference. CREON turns and enters the Temple with AMPHITRYON. The multitude follow. The POET and the WOMAN are left once more alone.

The WOMAN

I will not now believe that all is lost!.....

The POET

Nothing is lost! — for he was not the Light;
He was but one whose strength had momently
Uplifted in his hand the kindled torch
Whereof the spark lives quenchless in the soul.
Fail not in faith because the torch-bearer
Is fallen! — the sacred flame still lives in splendour,
Tho' the lax hand let fall the lamp that made
To our gross sense the glory visible!.....

HERAKLES

The WOMAN

I know no light but his, no faith but him.
He held the torch up in my darknesses;
He gave me light where the long path went on;
And where his strength made room, there was my
way!.....
Strong and serene as sunrise, I beheld
His advent; and, the little while he tarried,
The common clay I am of life's admixture
Seemed all suffused and interchanged with gold!.....
What shall my life become if he is gone?.....
And what is truth?.....and why are all the free
Fine faculties of the impassioned mind?.....
And wherefore has the heart such wings of faith,
Such springs of love, such hardihood of hope,
If he is gone? — I will not so believe!
He is still forward, still sublime, still strong!.....

The POET

Alas! Alas! I dare not hope — I saw
The Spirit labouring in him, as life labours
In one who dies too young.....The light was spent;
The voice was still! Alas! I know too well
The secret signs: — how often, in my house
Daily rekindled, daily have I seen
The light dying, dying, — the sacred flame
Burn small into the common day of life!
How often I — I also, silently

And suddenly have seen those walls, that make
The mansion of the Spirit's isolation,
Wear thin as light, and, like a prodigy,
The dayspring of the soul flush thro'! — till all
This mortal man was like a lantern held
Aloft, alight in the vast night of being;
And wayfarers might find their way withal!
I too have lit my candle at the sun,
And made my poems of it till the light failed!.....
Made only poems! — yet more than he shall make,
Who is grown dark as any proud glad man;
Whose light is quenched in passion and fierce deeds;
Whose soul is spent in purchase of this world;
Whose strength is small; whose truth is partisan!
Alas! Alas! there is no room for hope.....

The WOMAN

I will not so believe! They are not dark,
His eyes, where once my sightless eyes discerned
Spacious and grave nativities of light!
He is not, in the dust with other men,
So all inexpiably and weakly fallen
From where he stood, aureoled, invincible!.....

The POET

You love him!

The WOMAN

I?.....I dared not! Love? — O God!

I had not strength enough nor grace of soul
Nor grandeur in my heart to love him with!
Could I have loved him all might now be well!.....

The POET

Can you imagine of the human heart
Such prodigies? — that love could so avail
The soul once purposed to the ends of truth,
Which fears and palters with the price?.....Enough!
Let us go hence before the worshippers
Return to vex our grief and solitude.
Let us go hence.

The WOMAN

.....and seek for Herakles!

The POET and the WOMAN depart. A moment later HERAKLES appears, coming up from the city. He pauses by the Temple steps, gazing abroad over the immense prospect.

HERAKLES

I dimly see how far perfection is,
And what the utmost price of truth must be,
And how the strong soul is companionless.....
And I am heart-sick in my hour of weakness!
I have been much and soon and fiercely tried,
And now the process of the pregnant past
Yields to my sense its stern significance! —

EIGHTH SCENE

I was a tranquil householder, whose house
Of life seemed so securely locked and barred
That at the feast and in the pleasant mansions
How should he fear to find the fatal guest—
The Truth, whose voice sings out the wonder-song
Of life and death adventured to one end;
Whose eyes are clear, whose brows are pale with stars,
Whose nakedness is bright and terrible?.....
Yet, in the rashness of my discontent,
My hands, impatient of the tasks and toys,
Breached the blind walls of life's secure defence
And gave glad welcome to the ambushed foe!
Now am I pressed and overborne, as one
Beleaguered in a ruined citadel;
I am invaded, violated!—all
The doors stand open of my dwelling-place;
My heart is sacked and spoiled without reprieve,
For all may pillage in its treasuries;
The feast no more is spread but Truth is there
To consecrate the wine of human love
And transubstantiate life's daily bread;
And in the mansions I can sleep no more
Because of one crying "It is the Dawn!"—
I was a thrifty husbandman who tilled
With patient labour life's familiar fields,
And gathered in the harvest to his small
And well-approved and insufficient needs;—
But when the narrow bounty of my tillage

HERAKLES

No more sufficed to give me nourishment,
Eager of more superb prosperities,
I drove my ploughshare with a reckless hand,
Furrowed the fallow acres of the soul,
And in new soil of strange fertilities
Cast down the good seed of a great ambition!
Now in my soul the ripened harvest stands,
Waiting the sickle, — and my hands must reap
And earn perfection's lordlier livelihood! —
Leaving unsown, unscythed, unharvested,
The humble fruit of human happiness
Which was the substance of my daily bread,
And all my life long made the staff of life.
I was a happy lover, innocent
And candid in the paradise of love;
And love was human and was happiness —
Until I dreamed of the celestial Bride!.....
Then were my heart's inviolate secrecies
Disclosed — and I beheld her fabled face!.....
I saw how young she was and beautiful!.....
I knew her love's ineffable ecstasies!.....
And all the lesser loveliness of earth
Was in my sight no more desirable.
Then, like a bridegroom, heedless on his quest
If the dark way be strange and unexplored
Or if the bridal chamber have no light,
I hastened to my Paramour — I kept
Love's secret assignation with my soul!

EIGHTH SCENE

Now of that whispered, dark embrace is born,
In the deep womb of thought, a prodigy
Whose strength shall dispossess me of this world!.....

CHORUS OF RESPONDENTS
from within the Temple

We fear Thee and we know Thee not!.....
We know but this, when all is said:
That life is false and forfeited,
And love foregone and truth forgot
To serve Thee whom we dare not trust;
While, vexed with very sore distress,
We go nowhither in the trampled dust
Of life, companioned yet companionless.....
Yet still we serve Thee — as we must! —
Serve Thee and suffer and atone
And daily fear Thee and confess
The Kingdom and the Glory and the Power
Are only Thine — not ours but Thine alone!
For we are meek in spirit,
And live like creatures of the transient hour
Who dare not strive and suffer to inherit
The birthright of the soul, — who dare not be
Perfect as Thou art and, as Thou art, free!
No hopes may tempt us; and for us in vain,
Globed like a golden lamp suffused in rain,
The candid, living fruit upon the tree
Of knowledge, and the prime, pressed grapes of love

Which brim with sacred wine life's earthen bowl,
Ripen in sun-steeped orchards of the soul!.....
We are incurious, pious and afraid
And have no care thereof,
So the small price of all we lose is paid.
Therefore, as Thou art just,
Give and forgive! —
Forgive our trespasses, and as we humbly live,
Give us our daily bread!
By Thy small mercies we confirm our trust:
And since so much is forfeit that perchance
Man might reclaim as his inheritance,
Scant not to our desire
The mess of pottage that we ask instead!
But, in abundant measure,
Give us the trifle of our hire, —
The pride, the fame, the kingships and the gold,
The paltry profit and the hasty pleasure,
For which, to further and fulfil
The dark stern process of Thy secret will,
The soul, the truth, the strength of man are sold!

HERAKLES

Pathos — humility — surrender — fear! —
Starved, sterile, satisfied, supremely sad
Human vociferation and appeal! —
O frightened children, crying in the dark! —
Be well assured this hour of lamentation,

Of weakness and despair shall pass away!
Unconquerable is the strength within me — soon,
Soon to revive! — and spares not, neither counts
The cost!..... O I begin to be afraid
Of what I am! — for if I live at all,
I must reclaim the Birthright and redeem
The Spirit and the Truth from servitude!
Servitude? — then, the labours? — and Eurystheus? —
No, by the Gods, it is not to be borne!
And in the very thought of that abasement
Lies only madness and a black despair!.....

The voice of the POET
from below

How shall we learn to bear what must be borne?
How shall the heart not break when love is lost?
How shall life earn enough to pay the cost
Of all the tears, the solitude, the scorn?
How shall we not be utterly forlorn
When they deny us whom we cherished most?
When all life was becomes a dreadful ghost,
How, from such pangs of death, is life reborn? —
How shall we live at all?..... Thou canst not say,
O Heart, whose voice is lamentation! Where,
Where are the nobler virtues that repay,
When all is gone that gave us most delight?
When shall the soul, from what supernal height,
Witness the truth and save us from despair?

Before the voice of the POET is still, a very old blind man, led by a shepherd boy, appears coming up from below. At the same moment CREON and AMPHITRYON, followed by the multitude of worshippers, appear upon the Temple steps.

The OLD MAN

Is there a man who hears me? If there be,
Let him, as one who loves the Delphic God,
Straitly direct my steps —

CREON

Teiresias!

TEIRESIAS

Surely I know the accents of the King.....

CREON

Servant of Loxias, wherefore art thou come?
Thou, in whose sightless eyes the God has fixed
The fearful vision of all future things,
Speak, if thy words concern the fate of Thebes!

TEIRESIAS

Creon, I come not in the public cause.
Yet, I beseech you, guide me, that the will
Of God may be accomplished; and direct
My steps, that I may speak, as God commands,
His words to Herakles.

EIGHTH SCENE

HERAKLES

To Herakles? —
What is your message? Speak! — for be assured
If God is I will know His will with me!

TEIRESIAS

You are that Herakles? — O wretched man!

HERAKLES

Wretched?.....

TEIRESIAS

Most wretched of the sons of men
Is he who breaks the bonds of human fate
And dares the soul's transcendent destiny!
He shall, alone of all men, nevermore
Rest and arise refreshed from rest; rejoice,
Love, live, and have his happy human being,
As a man may, in life's familiar place
Where sleep is sweet and toil repaid and tears
Consoled and man's imperfect nature soothed
And satisfied, man's unambitious mind
Content, man's insufficient heart fulfilled!.....
For all his life is lost to save his life;
And all he loved is sacrificed and slain
To make love pure and perfect in his heart! —
Until at last, released from servitude
By long, incredible labours and the strength
That sleeps not, neither spares, the soul is left

HERAKLES

Naked with knowledge, where the lapse of time
Leaves its eternity unhazarded,
Solitary in a waste and desert place, —
Where once the friendly cities rose in towers,
And, rich with harvests, hills and pleasant gardens,
The humble paradise of human life
Prospered and heard no tidings of the soul!.....

HERAKLES

O breaking heart! — Is there no hope at all
Of any tolerable issue?.....

TEIRESIAS

Peace!
Hear me, for I declare the words of God! —
I stood upon the mountain, and the voice
Of God spoke in my soul, saying: "It dawns!.....
"My light dawns in the soul of Herakles!.....
"Faint and afar his eyes have seen the Light;
"His heart receives the gracious and divine
"Nativity, and radiant is his mind
"With rapture, and he hails the light with joy!
"He feels a splendour in his strength; he sees
"Burn with clear flame the torch of his resolve;
"The door of his deliverance stands wide
"Asunder in the vista of his vision;
"His hope is on the way; his faith is full;
"His winged ambition soars into the sun!....."

EIGHTH SCENE

HERAKLES

So, in the Dawn of Light, it was with me!.....

TEIRESIAS

The voice of God spoke in my soul, saying:
"Man is not saved because he sees the truth:
"He must be true before his task is done!
"Dawn crimsons on the mountain crest of thought,
"While still inert, disfranchised, unredeemed,
"The substance and the self of human being
"Lie far below in that sepulchral night,
"Wherein, like spectres moving in a trance,
"Like candles briefly kindled and consumed,
"The countless unambitious multitudes
"Of mortal men exist at all adventure,
"Timid and credulous of what they seem,
"Fostered or blasted by the winds of chance.
"Therefore, tho' Herakles has seen the Light,
"The long captivities of ignorance
"And pain and force and fear constrain his soul:
"He has not even reckoned with the price,
"Nor counted with the cost of liberty;
"He has not learned how much the flame consumes
"Which purifies, — how much the light dissolves
"Which shows the truth, — how much perfection is,
"To all imperfect, happy, human things,
"Ruin and desolation!....."

HERAKLES

Desolation.....
Ruin.....And then, redemption?.....

TEIRESIAS

Hear the voice
Of God!—it cries out in my spirit, saying,
"More light! More light! More truth for Herakles!—
"Light to dissolve, perfection to destroy,
"Truth to lay waste and ruin and make smooth,
"Make straight and smooth the pathway of the soul!.....
"Haste!—lest the saviour and the soul be lost,
"Man's birthright forfeit, and the soul's supreme
"Ambition bartered for a little thing!
"Haste!—and exhort the man enslaved to wear
"No more the chains of his captivity!
"There is no virtue he shall not forego
"Who fears and palters with the price of truth;
"There is no excellence or liberation
"He shall not earn who dares to undergo
"The mighty labours and the sacrifice
"Which win the soul's way out of servitude!"

HERAKLES

Where is the God who bade your steps come hither,
Your voice speak out the doom of Herakles?
Where is the God?—unless within the soul
Of man divinity resides unborn.....

EIGHTH SCENE

Why do you seek to cheat me with a phrase
And thwart my understanding with a name?
It is your voice I hear and yours alone! —
Blind, wretched Soothsayer — where is the God?

TEIRESIAS

Bear with him, Loxias, for his agony
Is more than mortal grief!

HERAKLES

Where is the God?
Where is the God? — if God there be at all!

CREON

Haply at Delphi, in his sacred house.

TEIRESIAS

God dwells wherever He is well received
And welcome in the life and soul of man.

HERAKLES

Delphi?..... At Delphi I will seek the God!
And if He is, and man may find him out,
There will I meet him face to face at last!.....

End of the Eighth Scene.

NINTH SCENE

Before the Temple of Apollo at Delphi.
HERAKLES stands alone near the steps of the Temple.

NINTH SCENE

HERAKLES

I left them in the quiet house — my sons,
My woman and my whole heart's happiness!.....
And all my life, and all my self that was
The world's great Captain in its little wars,
The pride and praise of men, I left behind!
Now, standing here by this prophetic shrine,
I am alone and exiled and bereaved,
I am forsaken, heart-sick, comfortless,—
I am resolved to read the riddle out
And search the secret till I understand!.....
Lost am I — lost! I know not where I am;
I know not where I go; — but whence I come
I know too well! — O this is all my guidance:
The passion to be other than I am
And realize self in the strict terms of truth!
The light is not — and yet the twilight is
About me, glimmering like a moonlit mist.....
And like a ghost I walk unreconciled,
Dubious and undetermined and forlorn,
Fearing the day, yet longing for the light!
O promised Dawn! — when you are come at last,
What shall your light disclose? — some spectacle

Of tragic desolation, — lonely days
And loveless nights and long, laborious,
Monstrous, intolerable servitudes ? —
Or shall I stand at once, as I have dreamed,
With all I love in the high place of Peace,
Dilate as with the Universal being,
Filled and fulfilled with your serenities ?.....

The great doors of the Temple slowly open. In the dark twilight of His house the shrine of the God and the veil behind it are dimly visible. The PROPHETES appears upon the threshold. HERAKLES turns his face toward him.

The PROPHETES

What voice of wretchedness and wild unrest
Cries out before the House of God ?

HERAKLES

My voice
Knew not the tones and tears of grief till now !
After a life of strength and high resolve
This is my hour of doubt and blind appeal,
This is my hour of agony !.....

The PROPHETES

The God
Knows neither lamentation nor unrest :
His calm perfection hears no human voice.

NINTH SCENE

HERAKLES

There is one voice He shall not choose but hear!

The voice of the PYTHIA

sounding in ecstasy from behind the veil within the Temple. As she speaks a CHORUS of men and women, worshippers of the God, assemble upon the Temple steps.

Before the House of God
They grieve and they rejoice
Whose utmost light is of the common day,
Whose aimless feet along the trampled sod
Tread the strait precinct of the public way,
Whose lives are like a pageant passing by.....
Within the House of God
No ear receives their incoherent voice;
No eye
Is witness to the deeds their days have done!
Like mummers at a carnival
They flaunt their scant disguise, and one by one
Go out into the dark in silence, after all.....

The CHORUS

Only a windy light no eye perceives;
Only a thrill of joy, a pang of grief;
Only a voice crying where silence is,
Where none respond and the brave song is brief;
Only the plaything of blind destinies,

Which ends in nothing as it once began; —
So is the life of man!

The PROPHETES

There is no shadow of imperfect things
Cast on the glory of God's excellence:
Filled with eternal light, His rapt regard
Perceives no grieved, importunate human face!

HERAKLES

There is one face He shall not fail to see!

The CHORUS

We live upon the threshold of His house,
And there like children sport with idle things;
We are a voice that weeps, a voice that sings,
A hand that traces in the senseless dust
The little hazard of our happenings.
Ours is a time for turmoil and carouse;
Ours is a time for sickness, sleep, and tears,
Labour and laughter, love and lust;
Ours is a time to come, a time to go!.....
Yet fearfully we feel, dimly we know
That all the while we live, thro' all our years,
Which run out, futile and disused, before
The threshold of His holy House, the door,
Dark with the gloom of unfamiliar fears,
Behind us, ever and alway,
Waits to receive us!.....Yet we dread

To turn our feet from the strait way they tread!
Yea! tho' our hearts, unsatisfied, are rife
With doubts and questions that will not depart,
We dare not ask or seek or knock
Or lay strong hands on the unguarded lock.
Rather from day to day
We cheat the mind with work and dreams and
strife,
We cheat the love-sick heart
With passion and blind love that perisheth,—
Until from all our toys we are taken away,
And in unspeakable loneliness depart!.....
Then, thro' the door of destiny and death,
Which is the door of truth's eternal life,
We men, whose times were squandered on the
sill
Of the soul's dwelling-place,—
Who found not virtue, strength, or will
To slant the door and meet Him face to face,—
Unborn, unwaked, unwise, and comfortless,
Pass from life's nothing into nothingness!.....

HERAKLES

Children of men, there is one voice of power
He shall not choose but hear; one fearless face
He shall not fail to see!—My voice shall call
To rouse the Lord; my hand shall slant the door;
Mine eyes shall meet Him face to face at last!.....

The PROPHETES

None can endure the grandeur of His gaze;
None can receive the splendour of His speech!

HERAKLES

There is one eye His glance shall not confound!
There is one soul His speech shall not appal!

The CHORUS

Behind us and before us
The shadow is,
Whose incommensurable silences
Never make answer to life's thundered chorus.....
And in our hands we bear the little light
Of life across the huge and haunted night
A windy mile or so;
And whence we come and whither we shall go
We know not and we fear to know!.....

The voice of the PYTHIA
as before

Yet may the inward eye perceive,
Hardly, and thro' the darkness faint and far,
Truth's single, stedfast star;
And learn, by vigil, to receive
The light; and, careless of the goal,
In the divine impatience of the soul,
Forfeit all hopes and fears to follow on!.....

NINTH SCENE

Yet may the heart's unuttered love believe
That somewhere the majestic sun
Of knowledge shines on calm immensities,
And drowns in light death's dark infinities!.....
Yet may the restless mind at last devise
Some scale and measure for the worth of things,
And rise, and valorously depart,
Led by the vision of the inward eyes,
Flushed with the rapt assurance of the heart,
Wearied and scornful of their parleyings,
Their dreams and games and profits, who before
The threshold of the shadowed door,
Build of base earth their human paradise!—
Yet may a man, at length,
Feel in the secret sources of his strength
The power to ask, to seek, to knock,
To force, if need be, the unguarded lock,
And, in the solitude where none else are,
To set the great, dark door ajar,
And live, and enter, and with words of power rouse
The Master of the House!

The CHORUS

It may be, as the Spirit saith,
That whoso slants the shadowed door,
Thereafter, deathless at the core,
Pursues his way thro' life and death
As one who walks an endless road,

Chequered with sun and shade, to some ineffable
abode!.....
It may be, as our dreams aver,
Beyond the door which none have passed,
The asker and the answerer,
The seeker and the truth, at last,
Are single and supremely one!.....
It may be, when the gate is won,
That whoso stands within the door
Exults with love's transcendent youth
In calm eternities of truth
Where, as with God's immortal breath,
The soul forever and forever quickeneth!.....
But we, whose lives are spent before
The threshold of the House of God,
We only know it is not thus
Ever for one of us!
Rather we know not what is worst or best,
And we are wearied, and we find no rest,—
And there is haply rest beneath the sod!.....
Therefore, as life has taught us, so we deem
Time is the little way from birth to death
Which flowers and stars and countless men have trod
And found no reason of their wretchedness,
No pondered justice first or last,
No light to guide, no Saviour to redeem!
So, in the passion of our heart's distress,
Our minds inert, incurious, and afraid,

NINTH SCENE

Receive the witness of the woful past
And worship at the shrines our fathers made.
And well we know, when all is said,
Tho' faith and hope caress their dream,
That life and death and sorrow and loneliness
Do something more to us than merely seem!

HERAKLES

O Children! — O my frightened Children! — Peace!
Children of men, it is not as you deem! —
Hear me! — I say life palters with the price
Of Truth's for-everlasting gift and grace! —
I, in my hour of weakness, I have dealt
In mean economies, and sapped my strength,
And vexed the soul's resolve with lamentation!
I too have feared and suffered! — and even now
I am afraid — I suffer — I am not strong!
I see before me with a black despair
The prospect of my desolation! — Yea,
And worse, it may be, if the worst come true! —
The prospect of a life's intolerable,
Infamous servitude!..... And in my mind
There is a kind of madness without name
Even to think of it, — and a red mist
Of blood drowning the vision of mine eyes!.....

He pauses; then speaks again. As he speaks, he mounts the steps and crosses the threshold of the Temple.

Children of men, I bring you somewhat more

HERAKLES

Than hope! Mine eyes have sundered darknesses.....
I have beheld the star of truth and seen
The sun of knowledge dawn over the soul.....
I have devised ascending gyres of thought,
And climbed into the prospect of perfection.....
I have turned inward from the spectacle
And florid insignificance of what
The rank world reckons as the life of man,
And set my strength against the shadowed door,
And come at last living into his house,
And called the Master with a mighty voice!
Him will I meet with face to face, and feel
His power, and hear His secrets in my ear!.....
And living as I go I shall return,
And bring you news and tidings of the Lord!.....

The PROPHETES

Forbear! No man may trespass in the House
Of God, lest desolation worse than death
Leave him bereaved and naked to the soul!
Forbear! — Inflexible as knowledge is,
Calm as perfection, merciless as truth,
So is the God — and no man may endure
His real presence and thereafter live!

The voice of the PYTHIA
as before

His Spirit is
Like a vase of diamond

Brimmed with eternal springs of living light.....
His heart of clear religious ecstasies,
Tranquil, transfigured, true humanities,
In love's grave gardens of divine delight,
Feels the immortal heart of life respond.....
His thought is spacious and serene
And like a consecrated place
Where knowledge is the soul of grace,
And truth alone is heard and seen.....
And who, with undiverted will,
As He is perfect dares to be,
And, in despite of grief and fear,
Has crossed alone the sacred sill,—
His voice He shall not choose but hear,
His face He shall not fail to see:
To him the very God is near!—
And, as his soul shall understand,
To him the Spirit and the Truth are close at hand!.....

HERAKLES makes a motion to advance into the Temple.

The PROPHETES

Forbear!

HERAKLES

Stern guardian of the Sacred Door,
I know the shining garments of the soul,
Which all must wear who enter in His house,
It well may be are robes of hueless flame
In which my human being and heart and even

HERAKLES

This rugged vesture of mortality,
Which tempers truth and makes perfection mild,
Must perish away and all be quite consumed.....
Yet is there that within me which compels,
And will not rest, and is resolved to go!

While all wait in silence, HERAKLES enters the Temple, approaches the altar, rends the veil, and discloses the PYTHIA seated upon the tripod. He disappears into the darkness of the inner Temple. A moment later he reappears, overthrows the tripod, and comes to the door of the Temple, dragging with him the PYTHIA. He thrusts the PYTHIA forth upon the steps, and himself remains standing within the Temple door.

The shrine is empty! Speak, false prophetess!
Where is the God?

The PYTHIA

Where else but in His house!

HERAKLES

I am alone within the House of God!.....

The PYTHIA

in utmost ecstasy

Melt in His arms! Resist not! Care not! Strive
No more, for He is quiet and merciless;
And by His means shall naught grow less,
But all that is shall greater grow!.....

NINTH SCENE

For, save with His transcendent life,
Within His mansions none may live;
And, as He prospers, even so
All thoughts and things, transfigured, thrive!
His truth is like a shining knife
Which slays, in sense and heart and brain,
Till what was perishable is slain —
And lives! — transmuted, born again
Dilate with His immortal breath!.....
He keeps no least account with pain,
With desolation, tears, and death!
Perfect and pure as knowledge is,
He has no private end to gain;
No covenant, no terms to make;
No silences
To keep; no death to fear; no heart to break!.....
Man's eyes are clouded with distress;
The heart of man is vexed and twain;
The mind of man is caged and caught,
Nor dares with lifted wings go free; —
His eyes are quiet as calm dawns at sea,
And single, and His heart is one;
His perfect love is pitiless,
And asks no less than all that man can give,
And will not suffer that man come to naught,
And will not punish or forgive;
His mind, like some majestic sun,
Centres the vast, expanding gyres of thought!.....

HERAKLES

Melt in His arms and cease from strife!.....
He wakes!.....He lives!.....The Lord has come,
And all is glorified thereof!
Melt in His arms! — and, for the larger life,
Forfeit the life you cherished and the love
That once was all your happiness and home!
At last the Lord of Love and Life appears,
And, in His being's excellence,
The little life of hopes and fears,
The little love of self and sense
Dissolve — exalted to magnificence!

HERAKLES

to the PYTHIA, almost in appeal

Who is the Lord—the God?—and where is He?—

The PYTHIA

as before

Who asks is answered by His voice;
Who dares advance is on the road;
Whose soul is free and fain to choose,
Has made the truth's transcendent choice;
Who seeks the God has found the God;
Who knocks is Master of the House!

HERAKLES

with a great cry

Mine is the desolation and the death!

NINTH SCENE

The PYTHIA

as before

Yours is the resurrection and the life!

HERAKLES

I am the God!

The PYTHIA

as before

There is no God but I!—
I am whatever is!
I am despair and hope and love and hate,
Freedom and fate,
Life's plangent cry, Death's stagnant silences!.....
I am the earth and sea and sky,
The race, the runner and the goal;
I am the part and I the whole;—
There is no thought nor thing but I!
Children, behold!—the East is white!
I see it dawn across the dark!—
I see the daybreak of the light
That truth has kindled in the conscious soul!
And hark, my Children!—O my Children, hark!—
For nearer now, and yet more near,
And still afar, and wordless still, I hear
The music of the soul's puissant voice
Rejoice
With festival in the heart and ecstasies
For man's deliverance!

Therefore cry welcome! for the Master is
Come to His own divine inheritance!
Cry welcome! for the Lord of all,
The Love, the Life, the Strength is come—
The rightful Heir, the Prodigal,
After long exile, now returneth home!

The CHORUS

Strophe I

Truly we care not for the truth,
We care not and we dare not care;—
But life and love and health and youth,
These things, we know, are sweet and fair!

Antistrophe I

Yet love is false, and life is brief,
And youth and health and hope depart,
And troubled is the human heart
With fear and agony and grief.

Strophe II

And why life is we dare not ask,
And what is death we dare not guess;
In doubt, despair, and weariness
We shirk the truth's unending task.

Antistrophe II

It may be that the truth repays
Thought's endless toil to reach its goal;

NINTH SCENE

It may be God is in the soul,
And wakens after many days.....

Epode

But we have neither part nor lot
With truth's far-sought and fabled grace:
Wherever is God's dwelling-place,
In all our lives we find Him not!

HERAKLES

Coward and weak and abject!.....O my Soul!—
How long the dark persuasion of my fears
Has wrought deception, and consoled the heart
With lies of some conceivable escape!.....
How long even I have dreamed false dreams of God,
As of some other than the self I know,
To whom might meanly, secretly be shifted
The endless labour of the soul's perfection,
The mystery of being, and the deep,
Unuttered meaning of the Universe!.....
Now, self-revealed, at last, and self-confessed
The Lord, alone responsible and real,
I stand defenceless, sleepless, undeceived,—
Naked before the truth!—What more is death
Than my bereavement and my solitude?
What more is death?—and what can death do
more
Than rob the Spirit of its resting-place,

Its refuge of insensibility,
And leave it outcast, as my soul is left,
Doomed to incessant vigil and unrest?
What more is death? — for what is life, indeed, —
The life I lose to gain death's larger life, —
With all its needs and greeds and appetites,
Its florid hungers, its satieties,
Its humble hopes and gross credulities,
Than the dark cup of Lethe to the soul? —
A prison-house, in whose captivity
The soul finds rest and slumber and reprieve?
And now, no more! no more! — O nakedness!
O desolation! O bereavement! — Where,
Where shall the Spirit now go home to rest
From vigil in the twilight of the frontiers, —
From the brave light and the persuading darkness,
The boundless solitudes and passionless
Immensities of the awakened self?.....
Where shall the soul go home?..... And, even when
At last the mind's abysmal darknesses
Fill with some huge tranquillity of light,
How, in that revelation, shall the soul
Find place and reason and the forward path?.....
Where is there rest or comfort any more?
And whither shall the tasked adventurer
Find respite or reprieve? O nevermore,
No-whither shall he find the breast of sleep!
And know you well it is a bitter thing

NINTH SCENE

To die — and in the thrilling solitude
Of death, to live — and labour, ever and ever
Afoot and sleepless with the vision of truth!
Life is a bitter thing to lose, and love
And home and wife and child and happiness
And rest and the contentment of mild joys
And small achievements and brief brilliant glories:—
These all are welcome and pleasurable things,
And bitter things to lose!.....And know you well
It is a bitter thing to go adrift,
Companionless and without pause or end,
Into the vast dark spaces of the soul;—
To dwell, sense-stripped and naked to the core,
In the chill heights of man's divinity!.....

The PYTHIA

as before

God knows, and I, who dwell with God, I know
Truth is a bitter thing to undergo;.....
And life's perfected metamorphosis
From man to God shall hardly come to pass
Save in exceeding travail and grief and pain.
Only in anguish man is born again,
Other and more and mightier than he was!.....
Only with strange and tragic ecstasies
Of body and being, mind and heart,
Life's human chrysalis
Is torn asunder, and ruined, and rent apart,

To loose man's winged divinity
Into the light of truth, the skies of liberty!.....

Yet, tho' the birth-pangs of the soul,
Which will live perfectly
With labour in its own eternity,
Are as the very agony of death,—
God knows no fraction of the human whole
Is there that wholly perisheth!
Rather in his regard, whose human eye,
After long vigil in thought's starlit sky,
Calmly enspheres the equable and vast
Clear circumspection of the eye of God,—
Who has gone on his way where none before have
trod, —
Who, in a single vision, sees at last
What was and is and what shall surely be,—
Nothing of all man seems to lose is lost
When man is slain in God's nativity!
O, rather, whoso pays the utmost cost,
All things in their degree
To him in strict accounting profit most!

The CHORUS

Strophe I

How, when, and wherefore does he profit most
Who pays the utmost cost —
Tears and blood,

Labour and sacrifice,
Anguish, bereavement, fear?
How does he gain his life whose life is lost?
For life is one and must alone suffice;
For life is brief and time is like a flood
Which no man has withstood;
And God is silent, and He is not here
To prove such ill things good.

Antistrophe I

How, why, and wherefore is it manifest
How of these worst things can derive the best?—
Joy from despair and strength from sacrifice;
Freedom and clear tranquillities and faith
From doubt and long, enslaved, laborious years;
And gain from loss and God from man and life
from death?
What can be worth to man so great a price?
Whence comes his profit when this price is paid?
When all is over and done, is sung and said,—
When life is waste and barren with blood and
tears,—
Whence shall the soul receive sufficiently?.....
What shall the soul receive for life's enforced
catastrophe?.....

Strophe II

There is no answer! God, if God there be,
Hears not our voice or hears it silently.

There is no answer save the one we give,
Who have learned something, since we learn and live,
And who are wise at least as men are wise.
Have we not seen the glory of the skies,
Felt the wide wonder of the shoreless sea,—
And made our homes on earth, where we must be
Whether we will or no?
Have we not learned in bitterness to know
It matters nothing what we deem or do,
Whether we find the false or seek the true,
The profit of our lives is vain and small?
Have we not found, whatever price is paid,
Man is forever cheated and betrayed?—
So shall the soul at last be cheated after all!

Antistrophe II

Therefore we care not what the soul may gain
Or what the soul may lose:
Theirs be the doubt, who dream! We take the plain,
Hard, certain way, and ask no great reward,—
Knowing how much 't is certain, plain, and hard
That by no wise invention or device
May we in the least measure change or choose
What our to-morrow brings.
Wisely we ask no more than will suffice
For life's least good and lowest reckonings.
And thus, tho' we are troubled with many things,
Yet to the soul's concern our hearts are cold;

Tho' cheaply, day by day, our lives are sold,
Yet are we cheerful with a little price.

HERAKLES

Coward and weak and abject!.....O my Soul!—
O God within me—grave and perfect Lord
Of life!—what passions, what rebellious tears,
What wild, weak voice of longing and despair
Have cried against thee in thy dwelling-place!
How have I wronged thy courage, strength, and pride!
What lamentable lies have lured my heart!
What chill of blind alarm has tamed my blood!
What sordid thrift, what weakness, what despair,
Have poisoned all my being with lassitude!
O human souls, my equals!—Well I know
How like a plaintive and impoverished man,
How scared and weak with old captivities,
You have beheld and heard me!—Yet, perchance,
It may be even a brave man in his time
May shed some tears for a whole high life's ruin—
And take no shame of it! A man may weep!.....
But God is in the soul! He wakes in me,
And radiant in the dawn of light, uplifts
A mighty voice of ineffable music,—wings
Of song that rise where, round the heights of heaven,
Cluster the throned beatitudes!.....Behold!
I am resolved to death, to tears and blood,
To desolation and intolerable

HERAKLES

Bereavement,— to the worst that needs must be!
And to the best, to new nativities,
I am resolved! And I will stand apart,
Naked and perfect in my solitude,
Aloft in the clear light perpetually,—
Having afforded to the uttermost
The blood-stained, tear-drenched ransom of the soul!.....
Having by sacrifice, by sacrifice
Severed his bondage and redeemed the God—
The God I am indeed! For man is slain,
And in his death is God illustrious,
And lives!.....And I will live, and sternly make
The grandeur of my purpose manifest,
And take my profit in the treasure-house
Of truth, where none may enter save the Soul!.....

End of the Ninth Scene.

TENTH SCENE

Thebes. Before the house of HERAKLES.

Nightfall.

ALCMENA and MEGARA are seated by the threshold in the last, low light of sunset. The POET and the WOMAN stand in shadow by the house-wall. The CHORUS OF OLD MEN are seated by the steps of the Temple of Hera, at some distance.

TENTH SCENE

ALCMENA

My life burns dimly, like a famished lamp
Wasting at midnight, for my son's return.....

MEGARA

My life burns, and my love burns stedfast!—clear
And calm and candid as a guarded flame
Of assignation and of sacred vigil,
Quietly in the casement of his home.....

The WOMAN

My life burns keenly, like a glutted fire
Set at the pier-head by a wind-swept sea
To be his land-fall and his harbinger!.....

MEGARA

Like flowers unheeded in a desert place,
The long days one by one wither away;
The long nights, still and stainless, one by one
Turn, with the wan, weak daybreak in their hair,
Dismantled of its starry diadems,
And, chill and livid as a lifeless face,
Pass—as the vast light strengthens and it dawns!.....
And day and night find me and leave me here,

HERAKLES

Where, solitary, about the open door,
I wait for his return, and keep his house,
And give his sons and mine lovingly bread
And care and welfare and serenity.
Yet, in despite of all I do, my life
Seems like a fruitful field unharvested
While he is far adventured and in peril
About such secret business of the soul.....

ALCMENA

It is the virtue and necessity
Of women, with such courage as we use,
Thus, by the threshold and the fire-light,
To serve life's large intent, and wait alone,
Strong and undaunted, for the man to come,
Who is abroad, eager with lusts and dreams
And pastimes.....Thus the sane and serious strength
Of life's true cause, in us exemplified,
Patient in us, prevails and shall prevail.

The WOMAN

It is the virtue and necessity
Of every soul to watch and wait alone,
Patient and faithful, till the Saviour comes!.....

The POET

Many shall come with gospels of salvation,
Mysterious and august; with ecstasies

And partial laws and rapt, peculiar creeds.
Many shall come, with mystic loves and faiths,
With strange conversions and perverted lusts,
With formal beauties and facilities.
Many shall come—the foolish, false and fond,
The mystic and the meek shall come — in vain!
And He, at last, — surely He, too, shall come!
And we, who know him not, — what secret signs
Shall prove him to our sense, shall specify
The Knower of the secrets of all hearts,
The single Truth Incarnate? — When He comes,
How shall we know the Saviour? — we, who learn,
With all our pains, such scant and partial things!
How shall His advent be revealed? What news,
What news for the insatiable generations
Eager of thought's transcendent enterprise—
What tidings of redemption and reprieve—
What chart, what guidance, what discovery—
What cup brimmed over from the Sacred Fount—
What apple from the gold Hesperides —
What irrecusable witness shall He bring
As earnest that His life has learned and loved
And served the soul's austere necessities,
And, for the liberal and resplendent Truth,
Made an eternal mansion in the Soul?.....

The WOMAN

Sternly and curiously of whoso comes,

Well may we ask; for He shall surely bring
The unimaginable and perfect proof!

The POET

Not He alone—we too must undergo
The stringent doubt! Well may we ask, indeed,
What tidings of salvation and the soul
Has any man after his Great Adventure?.....
Well may we ask!—for in our several hearts
Surely the selfsame question probes us all,
We, the Departed, who must soon return
To that strange nameless Nothing whence we came.....
Shall we return impoverished or, at last,
Rich with the truth's serene prosperities?
Shall we, to-morrow or to-morrow, turn
Into the sunset and the early stars
Brows branded with dishonour and defeat,
Or, with the sacred monstrance of the soul's
Excellent victory, elate and calm?
Shall we return from life dismayed and dazed,
Or quiet with an exceeding majesty,
As God is in His garden of great stars,
Where all things, each in its eternal kind,
Minister to the welfare of the soul?.....

The WOMAN

He is the Son of God; he is gone forth
To find his Father in a better place;

And he shall come with tidings of salvation
And news of great concern for every soul.
He is the Saviour: he shall fortify,
He shall bear up and nourish and sustain
All weakness, fears, and insufficiences—
All incapacities like mine, and all
Scrupulous infidelities like yours.
He shall return so free that he shall find
In you, in me himself exemplified,
And give our wingless, anxious pilgrimage
The audacious, free, far furtherance of his wings!.....

The CHORUS
from the steps of the Temple

Strophe I

Verily, Thou and I
And all men whatsoever who live and die,
We are of one humanity;
We are of one supreme infirmity,
One gross resemblance, one result, one cause;
We are as man has been before,
And no man of us all is more,
And no man of us all is free
And master of the inexorable laws;—
And all is always as it was,
And so it evermore shall be!.....
We are — who were not nor shall be again!
Yet do we vainly live and vain are we;

Vain is contentment and desire is vain
And hope is fruitless as a blasted tree;
Vain are the powers and labours of the brain;
Vain are the pangs that shake the human breast;
Vain is the body's brief felicity;
Vain was our youth! — and when the sober years
Leave us bereft and spent,—when more and more
We feel, upon life's darkening, lonely shore,
Violent and blind, the rising tide of tears,—
Vainly we seek for refuge, long for rest!.....

Antistrophe I

There is no refuge and no rest for us!
Tho' in a myriad tongues and ways
The old, wild voice of legend says,
"Thither He dwelt, and here of old He trod!"
Yet does the thought and the desire of God
Leave us impartial and incredulous.
For we have seen how all things pass
In sorrow, infirmity, and pain;
How all is dust that comes to dust;
How nothing is where nothing was;
How thick beneath the pleasant grass
Are strewn the corpses of the slain; —
And strive however much we will
We cannot find God's justice just!
How shall we call Him Father still,
Our Father, who returns us ill

For good, and when we ask for bread
Gives us a stone instead?
How shall we weep to Him? — He does not care!
How shall we sing to Him? — He does not hear!
How shall we love Him? — for He is not here!
How shall we know if God, indeed, be there?.....
Rather, by God forsaken and forgot,
Let us believe, at last, that He is dead,
Or never was and now is not!.....

Strophe II

Yea! to our sense, in life's fantastic trance,
Nothing there is apparent more than blind
Chance and mischance.....
We drift like derelicts with the aimless wind
Across the darkness of our ignorance.....
Our lives were kindled like a flame;
Nameless out of the nameless dark we came;
And like a flame that will no longer burn
Into the selfsame darkness we return!.....
Were we not then enraptured and unwise,
Should we believe
What the soul's secret whisper says,
And strive to find, with vision-haunted eyes,
Paths into Paradise,
Where we might walk with God in all His ways?
Shall we not rather patiently perceive,
And with an unambitious mind,

Man's witness to mankind
Touching these matters of the soul's concern?
Shall we not rather strive at last to learn
How, wisely and ingloriously, to live?
For we have seen, since human life began,
How inconsiderable is man,
How weak his mind's resolve, how brief his love,
How vain his strivings and his flights have been,
To find the freedom that he knows not of,
The light of Truth his eyes have never seen.....

Antistrophe II

Did not, of old, Bellerophon
Drive his winged courser up the stagnant night
To find if in God's house there was any light,
Or any welcome in God's house? — He said,
"There, in my Father's house, is home.
"There, in His love's illimitable dome,
"Are many mansions — and I am His son.
"And on my Father's breast
"There will I rest;
"There will I lay down my exhausted head,
"My broken heart, and there be cheered and stayed;
"There will I walk with God
"In the calm ways that He is wont to tread,
"Quiet and undismayed.....
"There will I live, and live no longer here,
"Blind and deceived! What else is there to do,

TENTH SCENE

"When all of life is questioned thro' and thro',
"Save with a solemn joy to question God and hear
"The splendour of His speech sing in my ear?.....
"I am the Son of God! — and well I know
"The Son can do no trespass if he go
"Hardily where his Father's feet have trod.
"I am the Son of Man!—and I shall be
"Welcome within the Paradise of God.
"There shall He bend the Sacred Tree
"Of Knowledge, and auspiciously
"Gather the ripened fruit for me,
"And strike the rock of Death, and spread
"The waters of eternal life, and break the bread
"Of Truth's ineffable communion!" —
Thus he believed, and thus alone,
Bellerophon,
Launched on the quest, superbly rose, and rode
All the long lonely way, almost to God's abode!.....
Till, at the threshold of eternity,
He turned, and saw, and could not bear to see
The veiled and voiceless vacancy of death,
The blind abyss of human ignorance,
Fathomless and immeasurable beneath!.....
His brain reeled and his heart failed! — Suddenly
He knew his own shrill insignificance!
Then, from the very sill
Of the Unattainable Place,
The lightnings of the blind and nameless Will

Struck him down headlong thro' uncharted space;
Until at length —
By the divine, immitigable fire
Sapped in his spirit's inmost strength,
Seared and corrupted to the core
Of love and life and hope and all desire —
He lay dying by the sea's lamentable shore!.....
Thus was it then; with man 't is always thus! —
So was it once with Icarus
Who eyed the sun,
And rashly took unto his spirit wings,
And dared into the darkness, up and on,
To find the secret and the sense of things,
Where, in the eye of God, all stood revealed!.....
But, when the springs of knowledge were unsealed
And Truth towered flaming on his sight,
His pinions shattered in the light —
And like an eagle slain in flight,
He fell from where day promised and dawn was,
Down the deep darkness, smooth and blind as glass,
Irretrievably
Into the all-receiving sea!.....

Epode

Thus was it then — yea, thus it always is!
Man is an eyeless worm whose chrysalis
Never, despite his utmost strength, is riven!
In no rebirth, no metamorphosis,

TENTH SCENE

Is it to man's imperfect nature given
To slough his gross humanity, and rise
Godlike, and walk with God in Paradise—
Free as God is, unconquerable and wise!
His mind is like a haunted house
Where veiled, vain figures walk in sleep;
His heart, where death's bereavements weep,
Where life's large, florid lusts carouse,
Is aimless, like a withered leaf
Vexed with love's vital wind of song;
The purpose of his soul is long;
The days of all his life are brief!
And since we know not what is death—
Since life is—since the end is near—
We care not who may come, we hear
No longer what the Spirit saith!
What tho' the Saviour come?—tho' deep
Within the soul,—as well may be—
There where the peaks of thought rise steep
And stedfast in eternity,
Truth murmurs at its fountain-head?—
We care not—for our faith is dead;
We hear not—lest our faith return;—
Lest we believe the truth—and learn;
Lest we believe the heart—and love;
Lest we believe the soul—and dare,
And strange disaster come thereof,
Of pinions shattered in mid-air,

Of ruin and desolation and despair!.....
Rather, since life is fugitive,
And truth's assurance none can give,
And no redemption makes us free,
We care not, hear not, nor believe! —
We live as man must always live;
We are as man must always be.....

The POET

It is not, up the shoreless seas of night
And thro' far twilights of the Mystery,
The rash adventure and the reckless flight
Of winged desires and dreams of liberty,
Veered to no lodestar at truth's stedfast pole,
Which can avail
The serious, strong, ambition of the soul.
The wings of man's brave ecstasies are frail;
The passions native to the human breast—
The secret raptures which persuade —
The unutterable longings which prevail—
Tried in the truth's tremendous test,
Prove weak and daunted and dismayed.
There is no swift and violent way,
There is no near and friendly goal;
There is a certain price to pay
And certain profit for the soul,
And certain justice! — when, at length,
Clad in the heart's clear, human flame,

TENTH SCENE

Phrased in the mind and conscious of its aim,
Man's inmost spiritual strength —
No more wind-driven and sea-spent
On the waste waters of his ignorance —
Interprets life by his significance,
And lives, and earns his true enfranchisement!.....

HERAKLES appears, almost invisible in the closing dusk of nightfall. The POET perceives him, and his song ceases. He leans forward, staring into the darkness. Silence.

The POET
with a great, sudden gesture toward the figure of HERAKLES

Herakles! —

HERAKLES
intense and motionless

It is I!

ALCMENA

My son! —

The WOMAN

My Saviour!

MEGARA

Herakles! —

HERAKLES

It is I!

MEGARA

starting toward him

My Love —

HERAKLES

Be still!

Stand back! Stand back! I know you not! The dark
Closes you in — while round me and within me
Abounds the perfect and perpetual light!
Stand back! Be still! I am a soul withdrawn —
Shining and stark!.....My strength is like a sword,
And like a fire, and like a fearful doom!.....
I have stood solitary in the place of God —
Solitary and august!.....I know my will —

MEGARA

Herakles! Herakles!

ALCMENA

My son! —

HERAKLES

Be still!

Crowd not upon me, phantoms of the past!
I am not whom you deem! — you love me not! —
You know not me! —

To MEGARA

I am not as I was,
When last we felt in one another's breast,

Strong at the core, the pulse of life abound!
I am a stranger — you are strange to me!
The eyes, the eyes, shining with love upon me, —
The thrilled, intense face and the tender word, —
The tremulous, great joy of the stretched hands
And the surrendered heart hailing me home,—
These are no longer mine — mine to receive
Or mine to give! — No more, no more, for me,
Is any human welcome in this world!.....
There in the Temple — there, alone alone,
I died!.....And there I lived again—and thence
I come — and I shall soon depart, alone —
Alone and nameless!.....Had you means and will,
Well might the Truth be cogent to your sense! —
But I am like a pillar of pure flame
Whose vision blinds and whose embrace destroys!

MEGARA

I love you, Herakles.

HERAKLES

You loved me—loved me
When in the plaintive dusk of life I was—
When I was dark and cold as dust! — I am
Incarnate fire! I am the Householder,
Who in the House of Life slept overlong
And walked asleep in dreams.....And sleeps no more!
And dreams no more! — Yea! sleeps and dreams no
more,

HERAKLES

Ghosts of a vanished dream! Bear witness, you
Who see me; you who know me not, bear witness!—
I am the Unknown God!.....And therefore woe,
Woe unto you all who hear me speak,
Yet understand no sense of all my words,
But love me for the slight glad man I was!
Press not so all persuasively upon me,
Lest you be rent as a wind-driven cloud!
For whoso comes across my purpose or
Assails my strength, he is by no means spared!
Woe unto you all!.....Woe unto me,
Whom the Truth's justice pardons least of all—
Who am not yet at heart invulnerable—
Who am the Unknown God!—and therefore, therefore
The scourge, the victim, and the agonist,
The Saviour and the stricken sacrifice!....

The WOMAN

The Saviour!—

The POET

Sacrifice?—the sacrifice?—
What shall I understand? O Messenger,
Is Sacrifice your good report, your news
Of great concern?—and how, in sacrifice,
How is the cost cyphered and signified?

HERAKLES

Ask me no more! Be still!—

TENTH SCENE

The POET

O Herakles,
Is it the lifelong Labours? O, at last,
Is victory prepared? Are you resolved
At last to take the soul's task patiently,
And rise by sure degrees from servitude
In virtue of that work there is to do—
Gradual and long and constant as life is—
By which alone the soul exactly gains
Mastery and manumission after all?
Are you resolved and launched? — O Herakles,
Are you upon the threshold and the path?
Is it the start of all prosperities
You herald as you say farewell to us? —
Who, in the prison-house whence you go free,
Having laid down your life for the true cause,
Watch you depart into the stern, straight way
And years of endless toil, with love and faith
And exultation and heart-breaking joy!.....
O strength!—O toil!—O sacrifice!—

HERAKLES

Be still!
Silence! You know me not! You cry aloud
To craze me with the past's fantastic fears —
Frantic insanities — Eurystheus!.....Speak
No more! I tell you, in the House of God
I stood alone, and there the man I was,

HERAKLES

Florid and perdurable and splendid, died —
Died to revive! — and paid in sacrifice
Once and for all the price of liberty!
There is no toil, no servitude, for me!
I, who by one preëminence of strength,
By one extravagance of sacrifice,
Have wrought life's final metamorphosis,
And thus become as God is, without bond
Or any taint of man's infirmities —
What need have I to labour any more?
I, who have known myself perfectible,
And dared and died, curious of consummations —
Died to the world, and in the soul revived,
Friendless and free, inviolate and divine;—
I, who have gone the uttermost way of all
Ambition, and resolved a strict farewell
To all less things than the one perfect thing; —
I, who have seen tremendously across
The ruins of my ruthless sacrifice,
Thought's stately promise of perfection bear
The ripened fruit of its accomplishment; —
What labours are there more for me to do?.....

The POET

How can the labours cease while life remains?
Life is the heart's occasion, and the soul's
Supreme emergency!.....

TENTH SCENE

HERAKLES

to himself

O patience, patience,
Desperate heart! Patience, distracted brain!
Patience!—

To the POET

O be advised, I say, to silence!
Man cannot dream at all what may betide!.....
Even as we speak together, it well may be—
Roused and released by some chance senseless word—
The universal Will shall strike athwart
Your crossed, frail threads of heart-sick human life,
And rend them all asunder!.....O, be sure
I am resolved! Surely, if needs must be,
I will make life stark naked as a flame—
Yea, void and ruined as a flame-swept place!.....
I say, well may destruction come!—and who,
Who else shall perish of it, save they whose hearts
Love has made vulnerable?.....What fumes of blood,
What savour of slain men, what reek of carnage
God may demand, I know not!.....

MEGARA

Herakles!
Herakles!

HERAKLES

You—be silent most of all!
This is a deadly peril!.....I know you not!.....

HERAKLES

Take away your eyes and your importunate face!
You are too curious of me — Go! Go! Go!
I say no tongue can tell what may betide.....
I am dead — and I have risen from the dead,
And come again to you after some days;
And I am other than I ever was —
And you I know not, and I love you not!
What tho' you were my dearest of life's best,
My love, my wife, the mother of my sons,
My very children, innocent and mild —
Natheless I know you and I love you not!
O, hark! — hark! — hark! — how the shrill demon cries —
Naming you with an old, persistent grief,
And tremulous, long lamentations!.....

MEGARA

Hark! —
Hark!—how the voice of love cries out within you!
Hark!—how the voice of truth and justice cries—
Naming your wife, your mother, and your sons,
Who know you, love you, and forsake you not —
And will not be forsaken! Who am I?—
Who are my children? — Well you know our worth!
Can you bereave them and abandon me?
I am no casual woman of your lust;
They are no bastards born of harlotry.
I am the grave companion of your life;

I am your equal — and your sons are mine!
We are the candour and the tenderness
Of home—your home!—and we are yours, are yours—
And may not thus be outraged and disclaimed!

HERAKLES

Why will you cry out in the darkness, words
I will not hear—O ghosts!—O plaintive ghosts!—
Ghosts of the vanished dream — the dream of life?
Why will you cry out in the darkness—when
The lightnings are at hand which shall dispel,
With fire and devastation and despair,
Spectres and plaintive voices and vain things?.....
Beware! lest you may learn how stern and strange
And violent is the just clear voice of doom!
Beware! Beware! You are the living sign
Of an ignoble bondage and a will
Too lax with pleasure and emolument
To rise to the sheer heights of life's occasion!
Therefore beware! be still!—Your voice allures me.....
You would betray me.....I will hear no more!

MEGARA

Verily, in the light of life's real need,
Your words say nothing to my sense. I know
My worth and yours; I know my sons and yours
Sleep in your house, secure in you and me.
Look at me well!—for I have borne your children,

And tenderly and with an infinite joy —
In nights of vigil when the exhausted flesh
Cried out for rest, and in laborious days
Of unremitting care and cheer and love —
Reared them to life and laughter, liberty
And light, and generous grandeurs of the spirit,
And exultations of the heart, and strong
Joys of the body; and maintained your house;
And made my life's concern of them and you!
Look at me well! — Will you abandon me?
Will you bereave me of my love and joy?
Shall I be left defenceless and despised,
Haply the prey and victim of chance wars
In which I well may come to servitude,
Sweat like a harlot in some conqueror's bed,
And, in a sheer excess of misery,
Die of a vile and self-inflicted death?.....

ALCMENA swiftly enters the house of HERAKLES.

HERAKLES

I know you now! — I know you as you are!
You would betray me — you would rouse within me
Passions and vile estrangements from the soul!.....
But there is of my strength sufficiently
Now to withstand you — Yea! if needs must be —

ALCMENA reappears, bringing with her the three SONS OF HERAKLES. They go to their mother.

TENTH SCENE

HERAKLES

almost in frenzy

Take away the children!—Take away the children!—

MEGARA

Yea!

These are your sons! — Will you cast off your own?
Will you forsake, will you abandon them?
What?—shall the sons of Herakles be left
Victims to man's injustice and the scorn
Of an oppressive, vile, injurious world?
What?—shall the sons of Herakles be bowed
By shame, by slander outraged, and by greed
And violence shorn and spoiled, enslaved or slain?
They are the sons of Kings; they are your sons,
The sons of Herakles! — Shall they be left,
Helpless and weak, to lose the throne of Cadmus?
O look upon us well, as we stand here!
And know our worth and power,—and know your own
Heart's longing!.....

HERAKLES

.....vile estrangements!.....stratagems!
Beware! Beware! Would you betray me thus?
Know that I will not be seduced, enslaved,
Corrupted and made captive by your means!—
And take away the children! — take them from me!—
Is there no mercy?.....Shall it come to this?.....

MEGARA

How shall we not withstand you, O my Love,
Since you do evil in your heart and lie?
Witness!—we have no selfish will with you,
But the pure purpose of life's sacred cause,
Here in my sons incarnate — and in me.
There is no stronger purpose, and no cause
More pure and perfect. Yea! we must prevail,
Since, with the strength, in us exemplified,
Of all life's cosmic and immutable will,
Now we traverse your madness and your wrong!

HERAKLES

The Lightning falls!.....Hear you the thunders peal?.....
See you the keen, swift flame striking to slay?.....
Nothing avails!.....Nothing avails!.....All 's said —
All 's over and said!.....and one thing is to do,
One violent and intolerable deed
Of Sacrifice! — till the white altar glows
Crimson and shining in the white, clear light;—
Till the salt savour and the fumes of blood
Rise in the boundless air's tranquillity;—
Till the relentless sleepless Spirit knows
There is no human shadow and no bond
To dim its Truth, to thwart its Liberty!

HERAKLES grasps his great bow and takes an arrow from his quiver.

TENTH SCENE

MEGARA

Why do you fix me with such bestial eyes
Of madness and revenge?

With a great cry

.....The children!

HERAKLES

Death!

He fits an arrow to the bow.

MEGARA

He will destroy the children!

The POET

He is mad!
He is stark mad!

He seizes HERAKLES, but is thrown to the ground, where he lies, stunned.

MEGARA

.....The children!

HERAKLES

Death!

ALCMENA

My boy!—
Herakles!

MEGARA

Herakles! — the children! —

HERAKLES

Death!

ALCMENA

These are your sons, your wife —

MEGARA

— your little children!

Mercy!.....

ALCMENA

Have mercy! — Herakles! — My son! —

O —

MEGARA

Spare the children! — Spare the children! —

HERAKLES

Death!

He draws his bow and kills the children one by one as they are crying for mercy.

First CHILD

Father! — No!.....No!.....

Dies.

Second CHILD

Save me! — Mother! —

Dies.

TENTH SCENE

Third CHILD

Father! —

Father! —

MEGARA

throwing herself upon the bodies of her sons

My children!.....O my doves!..... My children!.....

HERAKLES

Rather rejoice! rejoice! Is not the deed
Accomplished? Blood, the blood of Sacrifice —
The dear heart's blood!.....Behold, these were my children! —
These were my little children! — yet I slew
And spared not! God is not more pitiless,
More perfect and inexorable!.....Rejoice!
These were my children! — and she too shall die
As they have died! None shall betray me, none
Resist me, none persuade me.....

ALCMENA

Herakles!

MEGARA

O my children!.....O my children!.....O my children!.....

HERAKLES

grasping his sword and rushing upon her

Silence! Silence! Silence! — Death! Death! Death! —

HERAKLES

O let there be rejoicing, for God's sake!
Set the strong hand unto the sword, and slay!.....
And slay!.....And slay!.....

Suddenly he sways and falls insensible to the ground.

ALCMENA

..My boy!.....My boy!.....

MEGARA

.....My children!

End of the Tenth Scene.

ELEVENTH SCENE

Thebes. Before the house of HERAKLES.

Some weeks have elapsed since the close of the preceding scene.

MEGARA and ALCMENA sit together near the door of the house. The WOMAN sits upon the steps of the Temple of Hera, at some distance.

ELEVENTH SCENE

ALCMENA

I, who am almost lifeless as the dead, —
Who live — if this long vigil of despair
Is life — as he lives who was born my son,
Anguished and spent with ecstasy and pain, —
Have kept this blasted fragment of my life
Day after day by the disused, dumb door,
That if he lives and is not dead and dares
Return and comes out of his solitude,
Damned and defeated, shattered and diseased —
Who was above all men superb and strong! —
He shall not lack the refuge of one heart
At least: — and still for him my heart is sanctuary!
Where else, indeed, should he find room to weep,
Save on this withered breast that gave him suck?
What heart should be to him compassionate,
Faithful and fond in sickness as in health,
If mine were not — of whose essential blood
He was compounded and made quick and whole?
He is my son! —

The WOMAN

He is my Saviour!

ALCMENA

When,
When shall he come? No longer, as at first,
We hear him, like an inarticulate thing,
Dreadfully in the darkness crying aloud.....
He is alone and silent.....He is silent.....
He is alone.....How is it with him now,
There in the desolation of his house?
Is he become a speechless idiot
Who, gibbering, glares about the vacant rooms,
Inhuman, scared, distraught, day after day?.....
Rather, it well may be, the worst and last
Ecstasy of the soul's despair is silent!.....
Yet there are times in my exhausted brain,
When, with a sense almost of rest and peace,
I do believe my boy is dead......

The WOMAN

He lives.
He shall return.

MEGARA

My sons shall not return!.....

ALCMENA

The maniac and the dead return no more!—
Theirs is the better part!

MEGARA

My boys are dead......

ELEVENTH SCENE

ALCMENA

Only the dead are fortunate!

MEGARA

My doves —
My little children, tender and very young —
My children — O my children! — Where are they?
All desolately dead! — all violently
And vilely dead, abominably murdered,
Pitiably and strangely slain! — my brave, my strong,
Beautiful children!..... O my sons!.....

The WOMAN

He lives.

ALCMENA

Happily not!.....I will believe he lives
No more.....

MEGARA

He cried out like a blood-sick beast,
And slew them, one by one! — their father slew them!
And they are gone, my white and innocent doves! —
Gone!.....gone!.....I saw the dreadful majesty
Of Death smooth their still faces, and their lips
Were dumb, and in their eyes there was no light.....
He slew them — one by one!

ALCMENA

.....and we are left
Alive!

HERAKLES

MEGARA

.....and life shall never cease to be
A blasted thing, a bitter broken ruin,
An utter and unendurable bereavement!.....
There is no end to the abominable
Agony!.....They are dead — my sons! — and he,
My Herakles, my love, — he is not dead!
He lives and lurks within the empty house,
A mouthing idiot, crouching like a beast,
Sullen and fierce and frenzied in his lair!.....

ALCMENA

Nay, I believe, indeed, my boy is dead,
As they are dead, who were well-nigh my children —
Happily dead out of this desperate world!
Let us believe at least he lives no more;
Rather, with joy, let us believe him dead!
For then with joy we too might soon depart
Where there is no more madness and no pain;
Where, in the Silence, God's dominion ends;
Where there is sleep which neither wakes nor dreams.....
Only the dead are fortunate! — I know
Life is an ill no mortal strength can bear!
What man could be more mighty than he was?
What heart more great? what soul more excellent? —
Yet is he failed and fallen and overcome,
Body and heart and soul!.....O fortunate,

ELEVENTH SCENE

Fortunate are they who have died so young!
At least they shall not fall, like Herakles,
Out of a perfect and a prosperous manhood
Into foul pits of madness and despair;
Nor live to sit, bereft and blind with tears,
On the charred ruins of a wasted life,
As I do — who am mother to them all!

The WOMAN

Herakles! Herakles! — He shall return!
He lives!

ALCMENA

Be still!

MEGARA

My sons are dead!.....

ALCMENA

My boy
Is dead! — And I remember, I remember
How he was radiant and tender, proud,
Passionate, dauntless; how his eyes were grave
And clear.....And I remember little things
Of him.....And I believe a woman dies
When she remembers, as I do, such things,
Such simple, poignant, childish memories,
Of a dead child!.....

MEGARA

.....She dies, I know she dies!

HERAKLES

THE POET appears.

The POET

O theatre of perpetual desolation —
Scene of the soul's last tragedy — where death
And ruin and dread, inexpiable deeds
Conspired with madness to the soul's defeat! —
O dumb deserted house of lamentation,
Sepulchre of the soul! — and you, and you,
Mourners before the sepulchre, poor hearts! —
What can console you or redeem you now?
Nothing avails, I know, nothing avails!
For all is lost: there is no prosperous
Expectancy, no refuge any more!.....
Therefore I will not vex you with vain words;
I will but weep with you, and then — farewell!
Farewell, O broken-hearted women, rent
And splintered wreckage from the seas of life,
Stranded upon the sterile sands of sorrow
Beside the bitter, barren fields of death!
Here have I nothing more to do but weep —
Therefore I will not stay. Yet, O be sure
I understand you with a passionate grief!
For I — I too have suffered of these things
And shared with you some portion of your pain!.....
Yet will I say farewell, for now the long,
Supreme desire, within me, and the faith
That will not rest, revive: my soul once more

Animates to its own emergency.
Life and its endless future enterprise
Call me. I feel the longing in my heart
Of new departures and the liberty
Of open skies, great winds and solitude —
Of starlight on the mountains and calm seas
At sunset and wide mornings of the world!.....
Farewell, O dispossessed and desolate hearts! —

He turns his face toward the house of HERAKLES.

And you, who filled the measure of my hopes
Of man, and roused raptures of emulation —
Farewell!

He turns to the WOMAN.

But you — rise up! Not all is lost!
O let the dead bury their dead!.....Your place
And mine are with the living! Come away
Out of this charnel-house! Perpetually
Of all slain things fresh flowers and fruits are made,
When the new mind of man in the new world
Of thought's discovery tills virgin fields,
And the new future like a harvest blooms.....
Now is the ripe occasion. Leave the tears
Unshed, the dead unburied — come away!
We have so very little time to live,
To solve the secret and discern the light —
Such insufficient, fretful hours of dawn
And day and dusk in which to hurry on,

Home-sick and sick at heart, like strayed, sad children;—
And Home is far, and the great Nightfall comes!.....
Rise! Rise! The shattered lamp gives light to none!
All is postponed when death and madness come;
And we who live, we have no time to wait!
We face the Future!.....He is, with his peers,
Drawn down the sunless vortex of the Past.....
Bellerophon is fallen; Icarus
Is fallen; Phaethon is fallen; — he
Is fallen! Yea, immedicably his heart
Is cancered and his soul withered and spent!
And there is nothing in an idiot's brain
Save the unendurable nothingness of death!.....

The WOMAN
rising to her feet

He shall return! He lives! He is not mad!
He shall return —

The POET

— shattered or mad or dead!

The WOMAN

I say, he lives! I say, his mind is whole!
I tell you he shall come again in power,
Stronger and more serene, more sane, more wise,
Self-mastered, certain of his path and goal,
Radiant and unashamed, inspired, resolved!.....
He shall return —

ELEVENTH SCENE

The POET

You speak fantastic things.
There is no hope, no secret that absolves;
No mystic resurrection; no rebirth;—
That were too terrible!.....

MEGARA

Too terrible!.....
Here in his madness he destroyed my sons —
His children! Here he fell — he shall not rise!
Forever and forever his soul is damned;
His life is wasted as spilt wine; his heart
Rent like a blasted tree!..... My desolation
Is faultless!

ALCMENA

He shall never rise from this
Abyss, this degradation, this despair.....
O, let us all believe that he is dead!
I dare not think he lives! — for then, indeed,
Then, if the door were opened, we should see
Not him we know, my strong and splendid son —
Rather God knows what spent, deformed, dread thing,
What nameless monster —

MEGARA

— what poor beast of prey,
Blackened with blood!

The POET

What crazed, cringed human ruin! —

Suddenly the door of the house of HERAKLES opens. HERAKLES stands upon the threshold, calm, grave, erect, and strong. A moment of breathless silence. Then,

The WOMAN

with a great cry

Herakles! Herakles! My Saviour! — See,
My lamp still burns!.....And now the Bridegroom comes —
At last!

ALCMENA

rising up, blind with tears

My boy! — My son! — My Herakles! —

The POET

Herakles? — Herakles? — What miracle? —
What alchemy? — He comes, serene and strong,
Mailed in the grave, fine gold of victory!
Who can believe —

MEGARA

wildly

The lie is palpable!
Grim and fantastic phantom of the past —
Herakles? — No, it must not be! Reply! —
What cheat is this? — O what abominable,
Cruel, and senseless trickery is this?
His ghost returns — but where is Herakles?
Where is the madman and the murderer?

ELEVENTH SCENE

HERAKLES

I am the madman; and the murderer
I am; and I am Herakles; and I,
I am the Resurrection and the Life,
I am the Soul, whose inmost virtue is
Thus to outlive destruction and return,
Valid with Truth's perennial victory! —
Thus to survive, despite of life and death,
With awful strength, the throes of man's despair,
The unremitting madness and defeat
And grim disaster of his mortal days! —
Thus, with the flame of truth's unfailing lamp,
To light aloft its calm, inflexible way,
There where his human vision, blind with tears,
Sees only, in the nether gulf of grief,
Vacancy and the windy darkness! — thus
To pass with man thro' all the flames of Hell,
Till the crude ore of his humanity,
Purged of its dross, refined and purified,
Yields, unalloyed, its bright immortal gold! —
And thus, in power and splendour and dominion,
To rise from man's wild weakness calm and strong;
To sing in man's disconsolate heart; to find
Faith in man's abject infidelities;
To make of man's infirmities the means
Of victory; to be imperishable;
To realize God in self and strength; to save
And serve and strive — till man is overcome! —

HERAKLES

Till the immortal energy of Life,
Transfigured with its own divine intent,
Evolves still further to its perfect end!.....
I am the soul — the inmost, immanent,
Real and essential core of life —

MEGARA

And I? —
I, who have all my life long lived in love
And mild beneficent deeds and ways of being —
I, who am innocent, God knows! — shall I
Be as I am, forever a blasted thing,
Derelict, wrecked and spent in heart and soul,
While you, befouled with blood and infamy,
Rise like a God triumphant out of Hell? —
Shall I be damned and you be saved? — No! No!
Surely there shall be justice after all —
Justice at least! — since there is neither love
Nor mercy nor compassion in God's heart.....
There shall be justice! — justice! —

HERAKLES

In the dark,
I have endured your anguish; and my heart
Is broken; and it breaks again for you!
Verily, verily, in my solitude,
Mine was a mightier agony than yours! —
Were they not mine, the failure and the deed?
Therefore I know how mad the truth must seem

Now to your sense, as then it seemed to mine —
How mad, how dark — and O, how terrible!.....

MEGARA

Justice!.....There shall be justice!.....

HERAKLES

Truth is just.
And truth prevails, relentless and revealed
Between us: — I, the living; you, the lost.....
Only the soul survives — only the soul
Whose self and substance are the living truth!
Therefore am I redeemed.

MEGARA

O Herakles!.....

HERAKLES

Megara! — O my dear, I know, I know!.....
Love was your virtue and your life; and I,
Even I have choked the fountains of your being
And left your love bereft, and one by one
Shattered your heart-strings — till at last there is
No breath of music in you any more!.....

MEGARA

No love, no light, no breath of life, no being! —
I am a cracked flask whence the wine of life
Is drained away to the least, utmost drop

HERAKLES

Into the new-turned furrow of their graves!.....
You know not how it is at all with me:
I tell you I am dead as a quenched fire;
Dead as the dreadful eyes of a slain man;
Dead as the blue blank face of a drowned child;—
Dead as my sons are dead!—Yea, more than they!.....
Dead—dead—dead to the core!.....

HERAKLES

So am I dead—
I, who was once the man you loved and knew!
It is not I—it is the Soul, the Truth—
It is the God who dwells and reigns within me—
God, whom I am when all His work is done!—
Who is so sternly indestructible,
Who is not ruined and shattered and undone,
Poisoned at life's perpetual fountain-head,
Damned and abased and irretrievably
Crushed and corrupted even to the core of being
By this incredible, bestial infamy,
My madness fostered and my hands fulfilled!.....
It is not I, it is not Herakles—
It is the Truth, which has no heart to break—
Truth, which inures by labour after all!—
It is the Soul, whose inmost life and strength
Are of so pure and terrible a temper
That even against the iron door of Death

They are not dulled, and when the stone-blind eyes
Of Destiny shed lightnings that consume
The very being and heart and mind of man,
They are not seared or shaken or appalled!
It is the thirst and hunger of the Spirit
Which, with a longing so relentless, crave
The bread and wine of truth's communion,
That, tho' the wine be mixed with blood and tears,
The bread with madness poisoned, and despair,
They will not be denied to feed the soul —
Which finds its nourishment and lives and thrives
And grows out of great error by such means!
O verily, verily the human thing
I was — the man who once was Herakles —
After this wild, irreparable wrong,
This cruel, senseless, irremediable
Accident of my own infirmities —
Is dead, is damned, is shattered, is destroyed!.....
Know me at last, Megara, Megara!
Behold me naked and ruined as I am! —
All that makes human life desirable;
All that sustains and comforts and consoles;
All that the years can give from birth to death
Of perishable, profound, pure happiness,
And honour, and the clear, sweet, tranquil sense
Of innocence, and sane, beneficent deeds; —
All, all is lost!..... Yet when I rose at last,
In anguish, from the horror and abysm

HERAKLES

Of lunacy, scanted, despoiled, bereft —
A shattered, beggared, blasted man! — and cried
With a terrible voice for the inevitable
Mercy of death — it came not!..... and I knew
My strength!..... and clear and grave within, I heard,
Thro' the tremendous silence where the dead
Cumbered the stricken field of my defeat,
The soul's voice sound victoriously!..... I saw
The inscrutable skies of thought stand wide asunder,
Splendid with stars!..... And then I knew, I knew
That all was lost! — for man shall lose his life
To gain his life — and more than all was found! —
Found was the sense and source and strength of life;
Found was the way, the light, the truth — the soul!

The POET

Who can believe —

HERAKLES

Bear witness to the Truth!
This is the secret I survive to tell:
To him who hath abundance shall be given;
From him who hath not shall be taken away
Even that which he hath!

MEGARA

— My love!..... My children!.....

HERAKLES

Only the soul survives — and I survive,

Hardly and terribly enough! But now,
Now with a nameless sense of faith and fear,
Of grandeur and dismay and stern resolve,
I know I am invulnerable — I know
Life shall endure, life shall evolve in me! —
In me essential metamorphoses,
Phases and transformations of the soul!
In me new strengths and new validities!
In me conceptions, pangs, and pregnancies,
Labours and parturitions, throes of change,
Forms and conversions of the element!
In me new germs and new survivals, new
Mutations, new futurities! In me
Perfections, consummations, alchemies!
In me new life! — In me exemplified,
New life, more real, self-conscious and divine —
Perfect, immediate and complete at last!
I am the Life of life; I am the Soul;
I am the strength, the flux, the growth, the trend;
I am the future and the hope of man!.....

MEGARA

You?.....And my hope, my future, — where are they?.....

The POET

I will believe when all is justified —
Only when all is served and saved and done.
Many shall see, some shall proclaim the truth:

Who shall perform the truth? Who shall descend,
Wearing undimmed the starlight on his brows,
And, with the soul's serene, essential strength,
Toil in dark valleys of this human world?
Who shall perform the Labours, and in all
The days and ways and destinies of life,
Bring his perfection perfectly to pass? —
What of the Labours, Herakles?

CREON and AMPHITRYON appear, followed by soldiers and populace.

ALCMENA

— The King!

CREON

Herakles —

MEGARA

Justice! — Justice! —

AMPHITRYON

Herakles.....

The POET

Only the truth is just.

The WOMAN

He is the Truth.

CREON

Wisdom is justified —

ELEVENTH SCENE

AMPHITRYON

My son!.....

HERAKLES

The truth —
Only the truth is justified!

CREON

The truth? —
What is the truth?

HERAKLES

I am the living Truth.

CREON

turning to the people

There is no strength nor power but in God,
Children of Cadmus! — Witness and believe!
Him you behold is Herakles, the man
More than a man in fortune and renown,
Virtue and strength, resolve and valiant deeds.
You will recall how yesterday he seemed
Throned in a splendid, sole preëminence,
Pattern of men and favourite of Gods
And flower of manhood — envied of the world!
So was he once superb!..... Behold him now!
There can be now in all the world no man
So mean, so warred upon by Destiny,
So desperate as to envy Herakles!

Children of Cadmus, for that vengeance is
Of God and wisdom is denied to man —
For that the strength of Herakles was more
Than human, and his virtue and resolve
More than the virtue and resolve of men —
For that his soul grew emulous of God
And strove with God — therefore the hand of God
Fired his brain with madness, and he fell! —
Fell as a star falls, swiftly, and is spent;
Fell beyond all resource or hope..... And now,
Children of Cadmus, now behold him well,
Infamous, abject, desperate, and say
One to another, "This is Herakles!".....

HERAKLES

Say what you will, you shall not change the truth.

CREON

Children of Cadmus, witness and believe! —
Witness the will of God exemplified;
Witness the soul's expectancy reproved;
Witness, belicve, and learn — as all we must! —
Still to walk humbly in the fear of God.
So will I do — and strive as best I may
To follow in God's ways where they may go.
Therefore am I resolved — seeing, in wrath,
The hand of God heavy upon this man —
To cast him forth, unpurified, alone,

In the damnation of his monstrous guilt,
To wander in perpetual banishment!.....

A brief silence.

HERAKLES

Children of Cadmus! I have loved the truth —
I have beheld the truth — I am the Truth!
Once to the world and you I bade farewell:
I was a lover then, and the Beloved,
Shining afar, leaned to my soul's embrace! —
I was a Seer then, and in mine eyes
The visionary light kindled and cleared! —
I loved — I saw — I bade farewell — and yet
I could not go! — I merely loved and saw!
Love may persuade and light may guide the soul:
It is the work we do which shall avail! —
Only the work — the labours of the spirit
Wrought in the living substance of the truth!
Therefore I could not go when once before,
Dazed and deceived, I bade you all farewell.
But now, deliberate and determined, now,
Sane and serene, I well may take my leave;
For now at last I am indeed, indeed,
Gone from you all a long and bitter way —
Stumbled and groped and climbed, with bloody feet
And dreadful clutching hands, above you all!.....
It was the rough, dark pathway of my strength
Which was not skilled to any other road,

HERAKLES

Yet did not fail me when my spirit knew
Its utmost need, and which survives entire,
Inflexible and irresistible,
Nourished and nerved to new necessities!
I am become the vehicle of life's
Infinite aspiration — now at last
Shaped to its perfect, true, divine intent.....

CREON

Silence! Your brain is still diseased and dark.
Therefore depart, alone and unabsolved!

HERAKLES

I ask not absolution — there is none!
There are no lustral waters in this world
Can cleanse me of their blood or take away
The stigma of their murder! As I am,
So I depart into the future, so
I make life's issue of the soul! Behold!
I am the Hero and Protagonist
Of life, the Pioneer of life's true cause!
I am the Sacrifice! My purse must pay
The long, incalculable arrears of man's
Folly and ignorance and wrath and wrong —
The price of truth, the ransom of the soul!
For, as with you and all men, so with me:
The life my father and my mother gave me
Was all compounded of the sins and woes,

ELEVENTH SCENE

Passions and appetites, credulities,
Cruelties, lies, hypocrisies of man!
So were my home, my happiness, my hope,
Builded of frailty and the stuff of dreams.....
Therefore they fell! But in the abject dust,
See! how the soul's pure gold of truth shines out,
More radiant, more resplendent, more revealed
In the broad, roofless day of devastation
Than ever it was in the kind, tranquil light
Of life's content and blind security!
And see! O see! — into the light, the light —
There where before stood the safe walls of home —
What liberal, lonely spaces stretch afar,
Endless and unrestricted, to persuade
The homeless soul to new discoveries —
New labours!.....

The POET

Labours? —

HERAKLES

I assume the task!
Mine are the labours, for the wage is mine!

The POET

The Labours — of Eurystheus?

HERAKLES

They are mine! —
Mine are the weakness, ignorance, and lust;

Mine is the mean, harsh longing of dominion;
Mine are the crime and cowardice of man;
Mine is the soul of man — the self of God!
And there shall be no vile or violent thing
Left uninformed of my divinity!.....
Therefore the Labours! — for the soul must strive,
The God must serve, until His virtue is,
In man's degraded being and abject heart,
In man's deformed, incurious, haunted mind,
In man's gross greed and dull brutalities,
Illustrious and exemplified! — till truth,
Loved and proclaimed, at last is lived and known!
Farewell!

HERAKLES departs. The people, with gestures of horror, draw aside, as tho' in fear of contamination, to let him pass.

The POET

At last!.....At last!.....

ALCMENA

My boy!.....

AMPHITRYON

My son!.....

MEGARA

with a great cry

My Herakles!.....

ELEVENTH SCENE

The WOMAN
to the POET

Haste! Haste! The best begins!
He is before us — let us go!

The POET

You love
The truth — I see the truth. — He is the Truth!
Tho' it avail us nothing, let us go!

The POET and the WOMAN turn and depart.

End of the Eleventh Scene.

TWELFTH SCENE

The Caucasus. A lofty mountain-peak rising in pinnacles of naked rock.

On a narrow ledge, PROMETHEUS stands erect, chained to the face of the cliff. Before his feet the mountain falls sheerly away to green pastures far below, which slope steeply to a narrow beach of bright sand. The horizon of the sea closes the vast prospect. On either hand the trend of the coast, bordered by mountains, meadow and forest, field and stream, stretches in a vast curve indefinitely outward into the distance. Landward, as far as the eye can reach, rise high mountains clothed with forests and interspersed with fertile valleys.

It is a calm, clear evening, about half an hour before sunset. The sun hangs flaming over a windless sea and in a cloudless heaven. The moon just shows over the eastward hills. In the western sky there is one star.

The vast figure of the TITAN stands motionless and superb in the full splendour of the setting sun.

In the time elapsed between this and the preceding scene, HERAKLES has accomplished all his great Labours except the voyage to the Hesperides.

TWELFTH SCENE

PROMETHEUS

The night returns — and still Prometheus
Wears on his limbs the chains He forged in Hell.
The night returns — and soon the Bird of God
Returneth ravening to his massacre.
The night returns — and God is in His Heaven,
Throned in the world's dominion..... Once again,
As when I fared up the prodigious night
And seized the Torch out of His Holy House,
Round His resplendent Being in Paradise,
I seem to feel the everlasting Light
Blend with the voice of the invisible choirs
Thro' mansions of perennial festival.....
The night returns — and God is in His Heaven,
And fear and anger vex the heart of God,
Brooding on me and my indomitable
Rebellion and the soul's validity;
While far below men kindle in their hearths
And hearts the Fire I gave, giving them life!
These were my works! I have achieved, God knows,
Somewhat of everlasting worth and real
Significance! — God knows and life records
My hazardous and unalterable deeds!

HERAKLES

Mine was the cosmic issue — and in me
The purpose of the inexorable will
Of life, the process of the endless flux,
The motion of the universal being,
Found its assured, victorious utterance!
I was, in the beginning of the world,
Where there was only desolation, death,
Dismay and darkness, — where the lives of men
Were vile and violent like the lives of beasts; —
And I alone found out the Great Idea,
Found the supreme and secret meaning out;
And I alone found out the forthright way
Of man's deliverance, and restored the light,
And made of life a lovely and human thing,
And gave the soul divine and pregnant dreams!.....
Man was reborn in me! — and therefore God,
Jealous and fearful, came in wrath against me,
Binding me captive, whom He could not slay,
Here on this cliff, where His malignant hate,
Burning thro' æons of unrecorded time,
Visits me with intolerable wrongs.
Yet, tho' I wear His chains, and even now
The Eagle wheels aloft, scenting his carnage,
Still is my heart's inviolate hope serene
And undismayed; still life reveals its trust;
Still and forever I keep the Faith, and still
Bear and believe the testament of Truth.
The victory was mine and mine shall be

TWELFTH SCENE

The victory! — the first and last and best
Are mine! I saved mankind and now, in turn,
Man shall conceive, in his maturity,
My Saviour and my Comrade and my Lord!
Therefore I stand, invincible, and wait,
Solitary and august and unafraid,
As he must be whose witness to mankind
Is of the free divinity of man.
Therefore I wait — for He shall surely come!
And when He comes, with gospel on His lips
And revelation in His eyes and power
And liberty shining in either hand,
He shall not find me crushed and overborne! —
Rather, safe-guarded by the constancy
Of an unwearied spirit and dauntless heart,
Shall He, at last, as from a father's hands,
Receive the Soul's unconquered citadel!

HERAKLES appears somewhat higher up in the mountain. He advances to the sheer edge of the precipice and pauses, gazing out over the world. From where he stands PROMETHEUS is invisible.

HERAKLES

Hither away are the Hesperides —
Hither away is hope — hither away
The heart of life yearns unto Paradise!.....
Hither away the insatiable will

Of life, grown conscious of its aim, intends
New liberations, new supremacies,
New powers and new ineffable dominions
And new aggrandizements of being and life's
New utterance of the soul's new testament!
Hither away is the new enterprise
Of thought; the endless wind, hither away,
Strains out the sails of the mind's caravel; —
The stars, the sunrise and the land-fall are
Out in the dark..... beyond..... hither away!.....
Hither away love is a lovelier thing
And of more majesty and mightier:
Nerved to the temper of supreme ambitions,
Filled with achievement, flushed, immediate, fain —
Yea, all of profit and service to the soul!
Hither away is Truth more excellent,
Freedom more absolute, conception more
Creative, life more ample and lordlier,
Knowledge more vastly and serenely sphered
In new dilate horizons of calm light,
Faith more secure and Justice more divine!
Hither away is the New Future! — where
The harvest of the sowing of spent lives
Shall feed new generations, and suffice
To sow new fields and ripen and provide
The Living Bread of new prosperities.....
Hither has labour brought me; and away, —
Wise from the past with new proficiencies,

TWELFTH SCENE

Single and resolute and well-matured
To new activities, new avatars
And new validities, — the strength of life,
Spent all in conscious service to the soul,
Shall bring me on..... and on..... hither away
Into the Kingdom and the Power and the Glory,
Into the whole inheritance of man!.....
O not in vain have I been up and down
In the whole earth, and seen the imperial East
Whose florid cities shine under the sun
With banners and dyed raiment and red gold,
And in the wide, wild West wandered to where,
Round the scarped, savage, wind-swept verge of the
world,
The heavy headlands stand into the sea!.....
O not in vain, from the Iberian hills
To Themiscyra, from the Libyan waste
To the Thessalian plain, my feet have trod
The sea, the mountain and the wilderness;
My strength and skill have brought the outlawed beasts
Into subjection, and, with civil arts
And fine express proficiencies and grave
Liberal manners, cultured and endowed
With spirit and substance and significance
The shy, fierce lives of vagrant, bestial men!
O not in vain I served and sacrificed,
Loved and was lonely, and, in mighty works,
Extolled the Spirit, and practised and professed

HERAKLES

Tender and excellent humanities
And the victorious virtues of the soul!
And not in vain, out of the night of Hell,
I drew the Hound of Hell, the ravening Death,
Into the light of life, and held him forth
Where the soul's sun shed lightnings in his eyes
And he was like a thing of little meaning,
Powerless and vain and no-wise terrible —
While with my inmost heart I laughed aloud
Into the blind and vacant face of Death,
And cast him from me, so he fled away
Screaming into the darkness whence he came!.....
Nothing is vain of all that I have done!
I have prevailed by labours and subdued
All that man is below his utmost truth,
His inmost virtue, his essential strength,
His soul's transcendent, one preëminence!
Yea, I have brought into the soul's dominion
All that I am! — and in the Master's House
There is no strength of all my mortal being
That does not serve Him now; there is no aim,
There is no secret which He does not know;
There is no will save one, which is the Lord's!.....

PROMETHEUS

calling with a mighty voice

O unutterable ecstasy of hope!.....
O Son of Man!.....

TWELFTH SCENE

HERAKLES

Who calls me? Who is here,
Sharing my solitude?

PROMETHEUS

O Son of Man! —
O Herakles! — I am Prometheus!

HERAKLES

swiftly descending the cliff to where PROMETHEUS stands chained

Prometheus! — Prometheus! — Torch-Bearer! —
Titan! — My brother! — O my brother! —

PROMETHEUS

Hail!
Herakles! Herakles! O Son of Man! —
O Liberator! — O holy day of triumph! —
My brother and my son — all is fulfilled!
Yea, I have kept the faith, and all is well,
All is surpassing well!.....

HERAKLES

Prometheus! —
Friend and Redeemer of the life and soul
Of man! — O Torch-Bearer! — receive from me
The love and the thanksgiving of mankind,
Who keep and celebrate in sacred trust

HERAKLES

Your memory, living with the life you gave!
Receive out of my heart the love, receive
The emulation of humanity,
Which is the harvest of your seed! — for I,
I am of you and yours, Prometheus!
Yours is the light of life, the light of being,
In which I was conceived into this world —
Father!

PROMETHEUS

Behold, my light is everywhere!.....
Light — where the sun gorgeously dies away,
Aureoled with its own magnificence;
Light — where the quiet, interminable sea
Shines like a blind and burnished shield of gold;
Light — where the sky utters a single star;
Light — where the ethereal vesture, pale as mist,
Spun of the scant, strange silver of the moon,
Hangs on the shoulders of the heaven-ward hills.....
See! the whole sphered, smooth skies are like a bowl
Carved of a single azurite and brimmed
With golden wine, with light! — to slake the thirst
Of man's insatiable spirit, and rouse,
Far in the depths of his creative mind,
Light, the eternal light, which there displays
Commensurate splendours and sublimities
To these of God's initial ordinance!
O Light — eternal Light! O miracle

TWELFTH SCENE

And benediction — tranquil, tender majesty —
Spacious and grave serenity of light!
O meaning, revelation, breath of life —
Interpretation and significance,
Prospect and clear persuasion of the truth —
Impalpable essence of the universal being —
Light! — of the sun, the moon, the stars — the soul!
Here have I stood, — how long, day after day! —
Sole in my strength as in a watch-tower,
And seen, abroad over the living world,
The punctual sunrise and the stars return,
The light return, to me illustrious!
Thus have I been assured, and thus received
My life's recognizance — seeing the light
Witness my worth and vindicate my deed;
Seeing the light perennial, and the life —
To me and mine perennial victory!.....
And now, O Son! — O Son of Man! — O strength
Born of my strength! — I know not all in vain
I nursed mankind with mystic hopes and dreams,
And gave, out of God's violated dwelling,
Eternal treasures to ephemeral man!
I know not all in vain I have endured
These violent years and harsh extremities:
For you, conceived of my humanity,
You are my celebration and my crown,
You are my perfect proof!

HERAKLES

Prometheus ! —
With all my friendless, childless, desolate,
And lonely heart I love you ! Let us be,
Henceforward and together without end,
As brother and brother, blent in perfect love.....
O to surrender utterly — to give,
Utterly and at last and all in all,
The passionate proud liberality
Of the unspared, exultant, eloquent,
Abandoned, loosed and loving heart of man !.....
O to commune as equals ! O to share
The soul that finds no less than life itself,
And all of life and love and death and birth
And being its special issue ! — O my brother,
Give me your love and blend your light with mine !
What may we not achieve, who have so wrought
Apart and lonely — being at last as one:
One heart, one soul, one life, one enterprise !
Come ! let us hence.....

PROMETHEUS

.....O to the end of the world —
O to the end of time and truth, together
Let us go hence !.....I love you, Herakles !

He starts toward HERAKLES. The fetters restrain him.

TWELFTH SCENE

HERAKLES

Shatter the bonds! Rise from the fetters! Rise!
Come!—let us go in strength, and quietly
Blent in one meditation and one vision,
Elate, into the future, hand in hand.....
Come!—for the light of life clears and abounds;
Come!—the supreme occasion is prepared;
Come!—the victorious voice of love proclaims
The epic grandeur of the soul's ambition!
Suffer His chains no more, Prometheus!
The hour is now—rise and depart with me!
Will you be lax now the great door stands wide
Asunder, and salvation is at hand?
Where is your faith?—Alas, Prometheus,
Where is your strength?.....

PROMETHEUS

struggling vainly against the fetters

My strength has well sufficed
Here to withstand God's grim omnipotence,
Day after day, despite what agonies!.....

HERAKLES

Shatter the chains!

PROMETHEUS

still struggling in vain

He will not let me go.....

HERAKLES

Yet, tho' His strength prevails against me thus,
He is not now victorious — I am still
Stedfast and undefeated! It is well
With me! — for all the utmost power of God
Can rob me of my honour by no means,
Nor vex the heart's exultant happiness!

HERAKLES

Honour and happiness? — O hungry heart,
Dreaming of love! O rash, insensate hope
Of friendship and of free communion!
O stern, relentless solitude! — Alas!
Alas, Prometheus, yours are empty words!
What is the honour of a captive soul?
What is the happiness a heart can feel,
Whose love refrains, whose faith falters and fails?

PROMETHEUS

You speak at ease, knowing no fate like mine:
It is a happy and honourable thing
Thus to preserve so long inviolate
The life where human hope finds sanctuary,
And keep aloft the blood-stained banner of man's
Rebellion, like a challenge and defiance,
Flowing in the free wind of life forever!.....
It is a happy and honourable thing
Thus to withstand the very power of God,
And bear so long unspeakable agonies!.....

TWELFTH SCENE

HERAKLES

.....Thus to withstand a phantom, and endure
The anguish of a self-inflicted pain?—
Honour and happiness are cheaply bought,
Yea, for a little price, Prometheus!

PROMETHEUS

A little price?—this dire captivity,
These tortures, æons and æons long!.....

HERAKLES

The price
Is small, since it is insufficient to the cost
Of liberty, and has not paid the living wage
Of the soul's nurture in the coin of truth.
Life you have kept inviolate—and so much,
In all your captive and disconsolate years,
Was honourably done. What is there more?
What have you done with life, Prometheus?—
O you have treasured unprofitable things,
Lain sick and idle in the lap of dreams,
And wasted life and strength in senseless war
With vain imaginings!.....

PROMETHEUS

Nay, but with the Living
God!

HERAKLES

Who then is God, and what is He?.....

HERAKLES

Enough! — I know you, and I know your worth;
And I salute you and acknowledge you,
Prometheus, and your strong, magnificent deeds.
Here I salute and specify in you
The long, defiant life, proud and resolved;
The dim, strong, spiritual, heroic trust;
The courage and the unconquerable will,
Which held you stedfast in the urgent fear
Of dire, fantastic dreams and spectral things.
Yet, in the strict account, nothing is new
Since the beginning, when your splendid deed
Brought light into the darkness of the world; —
And know you well no splendour can suffice
Save for the moment's payment and reward!

The voice of the POET
from far below; sounding clear tho' faint in the distance

No single, excellent deed,
Born of the spirit's utmost need, —
No one magnificent
Stress of impassioned virtue, nobly wrought, —
No honourable and manly pride
Of an eternal conflict, hardly fought, —
No desolation where the soul is tried —
No grim captivity where life is spent —
No pain, no sacrifice,
No strength, no splendour can alone suffice
To pay the constant cost of liberty,

TWELFTH SCENE

The daily wage of truth's enlightenment.
Nothing accrues! — Of all the soul has been
And learned and done there is no usury,
Save as the Light is more before us seen,
And the occasion more sufficiently
Prepared — more grandly and more arduously!
And, save as we
Are — by the endless labours undismayed —
More apt to learn, more eager to become,
More prompt to go and more resolved to be
Free in the universal truth, which is our home.
The living of the soul is daily earned
And daily spent — to-day the price is paid;
To-day the truth is learned;
Yet is the labour by no means gainsaid,
For all is partial and provisional —
Yea, to the end of all!.....
Yea, we shall hear again the forward call
To-morrow; and to-morrow we shall wake
To find to-morrow's payment still to make;
And we shall rise to-morrow and renew
The labour; and to-morrow truth shall be
As strange and true and splendid as
To-day and yesterday it was,
The way shall be as endless, we
As eager, and the world as new!.....

A moment of silence.

HERAKLES

It is my poet, singing his soul away.....
Hear him, Prometheus, for his songs are sooth —
And all shall come to pass!..... Only, for you
All has been long postponed; but now, at last,
To-morrow and the labour and the truth
Are here at hand — and truth is terrible!
Courage, O Titan! O Prometheus,
Courage, courage! — you shall more need it now
That I am come to strip you of your chains,
Your lifelong honour and your happiness,
And leave you real and bare in the real world,
Than ever when all alone, incessantly,
You stood superb against the power of God
And took no ease of the remorseless pain.....
You shall more need it now to, gloriously,
And more magnificently than God, and more
With loveliness and with simplicity
And the sufficient, quiet, serious strength
Which He had not, who thundered and was hidden,
Assume — resume, perhaps, after so long! —
Dominion over more than ever He
Held under various rule of fear and love.
Courage, Strong Heart, courage! — for now, at last,
You shall recover what you gave away
Such countless vague millenniums ago: —
The Kingdom and the Power and the Glory,
The strength, the will, the clear eternities

Of truth, the sacred miracles of love,
The widening skies, the calm infinities
Of liberty — the inherent heritage of man,
So long estranged under God's usurpation! .....

PROMETHEUS

I shall recover? ..... My inheritance? .....
Mine? ..... What betides? ..... O what shall come to
pass? .....
Where is my victory — the full, the flushed
And mystic consummation of my dreams? .....

The voice of the POET
somewhat nearer

Courage! for thus and only thus —
As we are prompt and hazardous,
As we are rapt, religious and austere —
We are victorious,
And find the strange, steep way, and hear
The airs rush into song before our flight,
And pass out of the night,
Persuaded by a single star,
And learn that where the soul's adventures are
The truth's discovery is near,
And the delight
Of liberty, and pæans, and pageantries of light! .....

HERAKLES

Courage! —

PROMETHEUS

My strength and courage shall suffice,

HERAKLES

You shall be more victorious than you dreamed,
Prometheus! — for your victory is truth,
Only conceived in the unfettered mind
Which, of the gross amorphous element
Of life, in its alembic subtly fused
And wonderfully transfigured, makes the clear
Cogency of the universal laws.
Yea, God has long enough stood in the plain,
Noble and forthright way of man's ambition,
Wielded his regency, and for a mess
Of pottage bought his vast inheritance; —
And man shall come into his kingdom!..... God,
As truth discerns, is of the infancy
Of man — the primal, dim, projected shape
In which his anxious mind figured at large,
On the vast shadow of his ignorance,
His sense of the inevitable Unknown,
The chance, blind sum of nameless energies,
Amid whose secret peril he walked in darkness,
Bearing the light of life's concentred fire,
The pure, fine flame of the self-realized soul,
Fearfully on its way, windy with doom.....
For thus, in symbols, fables, parables,
We are expressed; we hear some vague report

Of what we know not, and our minds devise
Some image that shall well enough suffice
To methodize to thought's austere command,
To reason's quiet, inevitable terms,
The garbled jargon that the senses speak —
Which are persuaded of the Something there!.....
Thus rose the myth of God, when time was young,
When, curious of whatever strictly shaped
The horror and hardship of his destiny,
Man's fear and ignorance conceived the cause
In his own likeness, and believed — and wept!
Now we have looked abroad and looked within,
Straining the symbol, and we learn to know,
Quietly and at last, its secret sense,
Shadowed and insufficiently set forth,
Is, in the meaning and the truth, ourselves! —
We are the Gods! We are the Householders
Of heaven and earth and all that in them is!
It is your Self, your universe and mine,
Prometheus — yours and mine and man's forever!

PROMETHEUS

Mine is God's burden of the universe?.....
Mine the relentless energies of God,
Which lurk beneath this candid and benign
Masque of perennial nature, and conspire
To compass man's destruction and despair?.....

HERAKLES

I am alone?.....I am responsible?.....
O nothing, nothing of all my dreams comes true!

The voice of the POET
nearer than before

Brave, spiritual, and strong,
Let us take wings and will, O Soul! for we,
We have too long, too idly and too long,
In fate's relentless grip,
Lain like a derelict ship
Cast from the shining circles of the sea
High on the shores of time's captivity.
Let us take wings and will! — perchance
To-day, the least of life's impartial days,
In unpremeditated, common ways,
We shall achieve deliverance —
And wake, and hearken, and hear
The rush of the changing tide
And the shout of the flood returning, deep and wide,
Over the reefs of doubt and fear,
Over the shoals of change and chance,
Over the shores of time — and fcel,
Under our keel,
The old ecstatic buoyancy,
The strong, smooth, spacious, sun-starred breast of
the Sea!.....

HERAKLES

Prometheus! Prometheus! Prometheus!—

TWELFTH SCENE

The soul of man can never be enslaved
Save by its own infirmities, nor freed
Save by its very strength and own resolve
And constant vision and supreme endeavour!
You will be free? Then, courage, O my brother! —
O let the soul stand in the open door
Of life and death and knowledge and desire
And see the peaks of thought kindle with sun-
rise!.....
Then shall the soul return to rest no more,
Nor harvest dreams in the dark fields of sleep.....
Rather the soul shall go with great resolve
To dwell at last upon the shining mountains
In liberal converse with the eternal stars.....
O let the soul feel the unhindered wind
Blow out at sunrise to the dazzled sea,
Strain in its sails and urge its enterprise!.....
Then shall it tarry in the anchorage,
By teeming wharves of vulgar merchandise,
No more — but rather choose to go abroad
Into the great, gold morning, and afar,
Where, from new skies, new seas receive the light.....
O let the soul, at truth's persuasion, wake
And understand! — it shall not then endure
To fail and be at peace and profitless:
For little glory has it of all this world,
And all its strength is nervous and disused
In the low, little labours of mankind.

HERAKLES

It is alone and understood by none;
Its speech is not of vain, vile, violent things;
But on its lips the dominant, great voice,
Which is the one true voice, cries out in song
Of Lord-ship and a last deliverance! —
It is the soul of man — and can not stay;
It is the soul of man — and may not rest;
It is the soul of man — and will not fail,
And shall not cease to labour evermore,
Until at last its own infinity
Is in its own perfection all conceived!.....
Prometheus! Prometheus! — God is dead,
And man is overcome! — and you and I
And all men whatsoever whose minds report
The truth, whose lives exemplify the soul —
We are the Heirs of all the universe,
And of ourselves supremely, all in all!
Yea! — for the Lord, who dreamed of regencies
Too little perfect and resplendent, and
Set over them celestial deputies
In His own image, feigned and fabulous,
Is come into His kingdom out of sleep!
Yea! — for the hour is come, the Lord is roused —
And all is His, and all is victory!.....

A scant moment's silence. Then, his voice sounding like a summons:

Prometheus! — You are free! — Prometheus! —

TWELFTH SCENE

PROMETHEUS raises his arms. The fetters fall from his limbs. He takes a step forward to the edge of the precipice.

PROMETHEUS

Free.....

His face turns skyward. In the last, dark flush of the sunset the EAGLE appears, swooping swiftly down.

God's winged blood-hound falls to his quarry.....

HERAKLES

Your eagle comes as a tamed hawk returns.....

The EAGLE sweeps down and lights on the shoulder of PROMETHEUS, where it folds its great wings and remains motionless.

The voice of the POET
close at hand

And then! — O then it is, after the deed is done,
And the Great Gates stand open, and we are
 gone,
Who shall no more return,
Foundered and tempest-driven,
As drift and wreckage on the shores of time —
O then and thus it is we learn
How all the soul was skilled to ask is given!
And wonderfully and nobly we discern
A sense of life transcendent and sublime,

A knowledge that we shall by no means miss
The love, the grace, the grandeur that we earn!
For then and thus it is
The soul achieves its metamorphosis,
The Sleeper wakes within the House of Dream,
And, deep within the vision of his eyes,
In the starred, silent heights of heaven
The incommensurable night is riven,
And in the blinding beam
Of dawn across unfathomable skies,
His wings flash skyward from their shattered
chrysalis!.....
Thus do we end our exile; then it is
We find the last release, and rise,
Knowing the truth which testifies
That pain and time and long captivity
And life and death and destined circumstance
Are only phases of our ignorance!.....
And thus it is at last that we,
After great love and long adjournments, see
The pinnacles of thought lighten with song —
And all the spirits of the Free,
Calm and majestic, move along
In an ascending theory!.....
While we stand with wings and will
Nerved to the task before us still;
While we watch with stedfast eyes,
Clear and valiant as a bell,

TWELFTH SCENE

The flame of thought that never dies;
While we explore the secret none can tell;
While we prepare, in tense tranquillity,
For the inveterate miracle,
The soul's perennial truth, the truth's perennial
liberty!.....

Ascending from below, the POET and the WOMAN appear, faint and exhausted, on the level where HERAKLES and PROMETHEUS are standing.

The WOMAN

Herakles!.....

She falls fainting to the ground.

The POET

Love has spent its strength.....and I
Am hardly come so far after my vision.....

He falls on his knees beside the WOMAN.

HERAKLES

O human heart of love! — O Visionary,
Filled with the sacred utterance of song! —
Welcome! The hour is come and gone. Behold! —
Yours is the victory, for man is free!

PROMETHEUS

Free! — I hear Pyrrha crying in the darkness.....
And Epimetheus calls me.....and Pandora

HERAKLES

Sings in the total night desolate songs
And strange, old legends, dim with secrecies.....
I see Deukalion's face, fierce and afraid,
Staring aloft into the new, bleak light!.....
I was a thing of terror and of tears
To them — more sad and terrible than death! —
When, with my hollow reed of the pure flame
Of everlasting, living light, I came
Among them, flushed, triumphant, fabulous, —
Came as the herald of life's endless task,
With trumpet-calls and splendid exhortations,
Eloquent in my hour of victory!
I was a thing of terror and of tears
To them — my turn has come to fear and weep!
For now I stand in the beginning — I,
Prometheus! — as they stood in the beginning —
Pyrrha, Deukalion, Hellen, mortal men
And women — with the life they had not asked!.....
I stand in the beginning, stand and weep
Here in the new, bleak light of liberty,
As once they stood and wept, seeing the light!.....
I stand in the beginning — I, who once
Believed fond fancies of the mystic end —
The unimaginable, fantastic, dim
Apotheosis of my hopes and dreams!.....
I stand in the beginning! God is dead,
And man is overcome, and I am free! —
And who am I?.....And what is liberty?.....

TWELFTH SCENE

HERAKLES

Liberty is the freedom to become
Free.....

The POET

The soul's long day's work is liberty.

HERAKLES turns and begins to ascend the mountain.

PROMETHEUS

Mine is the long day's work..... Mine is the soul.....
Mine is the freedom to be free..... I know
At last and without question, suddenly,
There is no Power in whose almighty hands
I can lay down the burden of this world;
And I am all alone and utterly
Real and responsible; and now my house
Of life is ruined, and I am left alone,
Shelterless and at large, like a poor beast.....
All that I was — my value and my worth,
My sense and strength — is gone!..... The mind's defiance,
The heart's indomitable rebellion, are
No more; no more the tortures and the chains;
Honour and pride and happiness no more!
These were my virtue, these my hope and faith,
These were my own, my life's, significance:—
They are no more!..... And in the stead of them,
What is my meaning, aim, and end?.....

HERAKLES

standing higher in the mountain, in the place where he first appeared

To you,
As you to Pyrrha and Deukalion,
Now I renew, appraised and amplified
And more sublime, more glorious, more secure,
The one true, perfect, and profitable gift! —
All that there is at all I give you! — Lo,
Yours is the Universe and yours the Soul,
And life and labour and liberty are yours
To understand and blend them into one!.....
All that there is I give you, and no less,
And nothing more! — no phantoms and vain dreams,
No spectral fears and false expectancies,
No empty honour, no vainglorious joy.
These are destroyed — but not that, in their stead,
Other, tho' lordlier, vain imaginings
And awful ghosts and unsubstantial things
Should fill the shadows whence their shapes are gone;—
Rather are they destroyed that in their room
The soul of man may go abroad at last,
Gravely and quietly, as befits the soul;
And freely, masterfully and wisely dwell
In the waste, spacious realm, withheld so long!

PROMETHEUS

I understand at last. The end is come

Of all my dreams, for now the new bleak light
Of the Beginning is upon mine eyes,
And I am wakened!.....And I understand
At last.....And Truth is grave and chaste as death —
And radiant as life is in its whole strength!
So, as I may, I take the stern, great gift:
Mine is the Soul, and mine the Universe;
Mine is the burden, mine the task. I know
The price of Truth, the worth of Liberty.
I understand at last — and now my strength
Returns! — Where are the labours and the life?.....
Where is the conflict?.....Where the victory?.....

HERAKLES

Knowledge alone is victory! When all
Is understood, all is subdued, received,
Possessed and perfect. For the soul of man
Is, in the universe of force and change,
Of blind, immeasurable energies,
Subtile and secret and supremely one,
The sole self-realized power, the single strength
Aimed and reflective and perfectible.
Therefore alone the mind's conception turns
Chaos to cosmos, ignorance to truth,
Force to the freedom of articulate laws —
Giving to phases of the senseless flux,
One after one, the soul's identity.
Yea, of the soul is all our hope! To know

Is truth and freedom! — Therefore, O my Brother,
Therefore beyond us, in the vast Unknown,
Waiting the power and conquest of the mind,
Is the far prospect of our enterprise!.....
And should we come into dominion! — then,
O then, at last, when all is lived and learned,
Loved and received in its eternal kind —
When we are Gods and Saviours, every one —
When in communion and accord we dwell
As native in each far, impermanent star,
And in the inhospitable vacancies
Are welcome and securely domiciled —
When we are strangers nowhere in the earth
Or sea, and nowhere in the being of man —
When the long life of all man's endless lives,
Its gradual pregnancies, its pangs and throes,
Its countless multitudes of perished Gods
And outworn forms and spent humanities, —
When all the cosmic process of the past
Stands in the immediate compass of our minds —
When all is present to us and all is known,
Even to the least, even to the uttermost,
Even to the first and last — when, over all,
The widening circles of our thought expand
To infinite horizons everywhere —
Then, tenoned in our foothold on the still,
Supernal, central pinnacle of being,
Shall we not look abroad and look within,

TWELFTH SCENE

Over the total Universe, the vast,
Complex and vital sum of force and form,
And say, in one, sufficient utterance,
The single, whole, transcendent Truth, — "I am!"

A brief silence.

The POET

rising to his feet

Come! I will lead you down, Prometheus!

PROMETHEUS

Down.....
My Son! — My Brother! — must we say farewell?

HERAKLES

Hither away are the Hesperides.....

The POET

Come! I will lead you down, Prometheus, down,
Where, in reality, in deed, in truth,
Your work begins!

PROMETHEUS

Where does the work begin?

HERAKLES

There, wheresoever the soul's dominion ends!

For a moment no one moves. Then PROMETHEUS slowly gathers the WOMAN in his huge arms, and begins to descend the mountain, the POET leading the way. The last vestige of sunset is gone. The night is calm and perfect. The thin figure of the POET and the vast stature of the TITAN, with the insensible WOMAN upon his breast, and the great EAGLE still perched upon his shoulder, loom vaguely in the still moonlight. HERAKLES stands motionless on his eminence,—clear, strong, and solitary against the stars.

The End.

The Riverside Press
CAMBRIDGE . MASSACHUSETTS
U . S . A

www.ingramcontent.com/pod-product-compliance
Lightning Source LLC
LaVergne TN
LVHW010226110826
845151LV00004B/1195

* 9 7 8 1 4 2 5 5 2 5 6 7 5 *